Translation Theories Explained

Translation Theories Explained is a series designed to respond to the profound plurality of contemporary translation studies. There are many problems to be solved, many possible approaches that can be drawn from neighbouring disciplines, and several strong language-bound traditions plagued by the paradoxical fact that some of the key theoretical texts have yet to be translated.

Recognizing this plurality as both a strength and a potential shortcoming, the series provides a format where different approaches can be compared, their virtues assessed, and mutual blind spots overcome. There will also be scope for introductions to specific areas of translation practice. Students and scholars may thus gain comprehensive awareness of the work being done beyond local or endemic frames.

Most volumes in the series place a general approach within its historical context, giving examples to illustrate the main ideas, summarizing the most significant debates and opening perspectives for future work. The authors have been selected not only because of their command of a particular approach but also in view of their openness to alternatives and their willingness to discuss criticisms. In every respect the emphasis is on explaining the essential points as clearly and as concisely as possible, using numerous examples and providing glossaries of the main technical terms.

The series should prove particularly useful to students dealing with translation theories for the first time, to teachers seeking to stimulate critical reflection, and to scholars looking for a succinct overview of the field's present and future.

Anthony Pym
Series Editor

Cover Design

Three Cubes without Space

by Ahmed Moustafa

Courtesy of the artist

Translation and Language

Linguistic Theories Explained

Peter Fawcett

St JEROME

PUBLISHING

Manchester, UK

First published 1997 by

St. Jerome Publishing
2 Maple Road West, Brooklands
Manchester, United Kingdom
Fax +44 161 905 3498

stjerome@compuserve.com
http://www.mcc.ac.uk/stjerome

ISBN 1-900650-07-X
ISSN 1365-0513

Printed and bound in Great Britain by
St. Edmundsbury Press Ltd, Bury St Edmunds, Suffolk

Cover design by Steve Fieldhouse, Oldham, UK (+44 161 620 2263)

British Library Catalguing in Publication Data
A catalogue record for this book is available from the British Library.

Library of Congress Cataloging in Publication Data
A catalogue record of this book is available from the Library of Congress.

Contents

Foreword

This book is about the love-hate relationship between linguistics and translation theory. Many linguists have no interest in translation theory, and some translation theorists are increasingly declaring that linguistics has nothing to offer their discipline. The author of this book does not entirely share this sceptical attitude towards linguistics; he does not see linguistics as the grand liberator or the great oppressor of translation studies; he believes rather that there are many things in translation which can only be described and explained by linguistics. Further, a translator who lacks at least a basic knowledge of linguistics is somebody who is working with an incomplete toolkit.

Since what might be called the 'heroic age' of linguistically-oriented translation studies extended from the mid-1950s to the mid-1980s, it is only right that these classic texts receive their due attention in these pages. However, in spite of the scepticism alluded to above, there is continued and even renewed interest in linguistic approaches to translation studies. We shall thus also look at these more recent developments, especially in the later chapters.

In relation to some of these developments, the author may seem to take a sceptical attitude. But that should be taken not as hostility so much as an indication that these approaches have not yet made their point convincingly, and that more research needs to be done.

Indeed, a phrase encountered frequently and with variations in these later chapters is: 'little is known about this as yet'. There are many areas of translation studies where much more linguistic research is needed. There has been a tendency for translation theorists to make a proposal and then pass on, leaving the ground largely unbroken. Other researchers have to get out their spades and start digging. One hope, therefore, is that this book will point the way to such areas.

In an introductory book of this length it is not possible to cover all aspects of the relationship between linguistics and translation theory. I have nevertheless tried to cover in reasonable detail those areas which have been central to the subject and give at least a mention to others, which the reader can follow up through the bibliography.

All translations of quotations are my own.

1. Introduction

A troubled relationship

Modern linguistics began in the early twentieth century with the work of the Swiss linguist Ferdinand de Saussure. He focused on the notion of language as a system at a given moment in time (a synchronic approach) at a highly abstract level that uncovered powerful principles about the way in which language in general is structured. The structuralist model he produced was to prove immensely influential when, much later, it was taken up by anthropologists, literary critics and philosophers as the one model that would apparently explain what we had always wanted to know about life, the universe and everything.

Since linguistics is the study of language and has produced such powerful and productive theories about how language works, and since translation is a language activity, it would seem only common sense to think that the first had something to say about the second. Indeed in 1965 the British scholar John Catford opened his book *A Linguistic Theory of Translation* with the words: "Clearly, then, any theory of translation must draw upon a theory of language – a general linguistic theory". In exactly the same year, however, the famous American theoretical linguist Noam Chomsky was rather more sceptical about the implications of his own theory for translation, saying that his theory "does not, for example, imply that there must be some reasonable procedure for translating between languages" (1965:30). Although no expert in translation, Chomsky nonetheless divined that there was something about the activity that put it beyond reason. Perhaps he had read what the academic Ivor Richards (1953:250) said about translation: "We have here indeed what may very probably be the most complex type of event yet produced in the evolution of the cosmos".

This uncertain relationship between linguistics and translation theory continued to be reflected in the literature. Eight years after Catford's and Chomsky's pronouncements, the German theorist Jörn Albrecht (1973:1) expressed regret and astonishment that linguists had not studied translation; yet the Soviet linguist Aleksandr Shveitser, writing in the same year (although quoted here from the later German translation), made the opposite claim: many linguists had long since decided translation could indeed be an object of linguistic study (1987:13). He rejected the idea that linguistics can explain only the lowest levels of translation activity, saying this was based on too narrow a view of linguistics. He did, however, refer briefly to the furore caused by the first major attempt by a Russian scholar to produce a

1

linguistic description of translation (Fedorov 1953), which provoked lively polemic and liberal accusations of 'deviation' (see Cary 1957:187).

The intervening years have not resolved the tension. Almost thirty years after the Catford-Chomsky declarations, the English academic Roger Bell (1989:xv) claimed that translation theorists and linguists were still going their own separate ways. The French scholar Maurice Pergnier has pointed out that even though linguistics has developed in ways that make it much more relevant to the concerns of translation, there are still those who would like to liberate translation completely from its sway (1993:9). Indeed, his compatriot Marianne Lederer is just one among many who dismisses linguistics from translation studies: "I hope in this way to bring out the reasons why translation must be dealt with on a level other than the linguistic" (1994:87).

Such a position is provocatively extreme. Linguistics quite clearly does have something to offer the study of translation, and in these pages we shall be exploring what that is. At the same time, however, we shall be pointing out the limitations of the discipline, especially if people want to see translation as an *entirely* linguistic activity or want to use linguistics as a recipe giving ready-made solutions to specific translation problems rather than as a resource for extrapolating general problem-solving techniques from specific concrete problems.

The relationship of linguistics to translation can be twofold: one can apply the findings of linguistics to the practice of translation, and one can have a *linguistic* theory of translation, as opposed, say, to a literary, economic or psychological theory of translation.

In the first approach, a subdivision of linguistics such as sociolinguistics might have something to say about the way in which language varies in relation to social status, age, gender and so on. It will enable us to recognize these variations and describe them. And when we have to deal with sociolinguistic variation in a text to be translated, linguistics can provide one input in deciding how to cope with the situation.

In the second approach, rather than applying linguistic theory to elements within the text to be translated, one can apply it to the entire concept of translation itself. Thus the theory of dynamic equivalence put forward by the American scholar Eugene Nida, which we consider below, can actually be seen as nothing less than a sociolinguistics of translation, describing the way translators can adapt texts to the needs of a different audience in the same way we all adjust our language to suit the people we are talking to.

Both of these approaches are found in writings on linguistics and translation, and we shall try to signal them as we go along. For the remainder of this chapter we shall follow the first approach, giving an overview of the basic concepts and main divisions in structural linguistics to see how important they are in translation, then coming back to them in greater detail in later chapters.

Langue/parole

Saussure made it possible to see language as a set of structured systems rather than a ragbag of bits and pieces. Some parts of language, such as grammar, have always been thought of as systems, of course. But the structuralist linguistics that emerged from Saussure's work attempted to uncover the systematic and structured nature of other parts of language: the sound system (phonetics and phonemics), the grammar system (syntax, which is word order, and morphology, which is word shape) and the meaning system (semantics).

For linguistics to make progress in describing these systems, Saussure thought it necessary to distinguish between what he called 'langue' and 'parole' (the terms are often used in their French form in other languages, because, ironically, it can be difficult to find translation equivalents). This is the difference between the abstract language system (langue or 'a language'), which Saussure saw as the object of linguistics, and actual uses of language (parole or 'speaking'), which were thought to be too variable for systematic, 'scientific' study because the factors involved were too numerous and too random.

An example might illustrate this: After a certain amount of alcoholic intake you might say *I've got a shore head* when you mean *sore head*. Now, although linguistics can describe the difference between *s* and *sh* in phonemic theory, in this particular case the difference has no *linguistic* meaning; it is a matter of parole; it is a one-off event that has no function in the language system. By contrast, the difference between *sore* and *shore* in the non-alcoholic *I got a bit sore sitting on the shore* does have a function in the language system: the sound opposition in this case serves to mark out a change in meaning, and it does so on a systematic basis (single/shingle, sin/ shin etc.) These differences are a matter of langue.

This distinction between langue and parole, and the insistence that linguistics should study only langue, led to tremendous progress in the discipline. Yet the early linguistic approaches to translation that tried to follow the same line led to considerable dissatisfaction. To many translators and translation theorists the findings seemed sterile, leaving out many things of interest to translation. The German scholar Dieter Stein (1980), for example, went so far as to declare that the linguistics of langue had little or nothing to offer translation studies (which is to forget that language structure can be a serious problem in translation).

The langue-oriented approach can certainly produce useful compara-tive descriptions of language systems, and, as the Canadian translation theorist Jean Delisle says, such things must be a part of every translator's knowledge (1988:78). I can scarcely envisage being a translator if I don't have that basic command of my languages. But these things by no means exhaust the problems of translation. They belong to what the German theo-rist Werner Koller (1979:185) calls 'foreign language competence', knowledge that is basic to, but not the whole of, 'translator competence', because simply knowing two languages is not all that is needed to be a translator, as these pages will make abundantly clear.

Stein advocated what he called the 'Sit/Text' approach, which involved data of a textual and situational nature. This would require a linguistics of parole rather than of langue and would allow us to account for such things as the drunkard's *shore head*, which is vital for translation. The French theorist Jean-René Ladmiral also claimed that "translation is a communi-cation operation guaranteeing identity of parole through differences of langues" (1979:223), while Albrecht reminded us that "what is being trans-lated are not 'codes' or languages but 'messages' or texts" (1973:26), in other words parole not langue. For Koller (1979:183), translation theory is "a science of *parole*".

The problem was that parole-oriented linguistics was scarcely developed. There was thus a fear that abandoning the langue-oriented approach would mean giving up any attempt to turn translation theory into a scientific theory that would rescue it from the earlier dilettante approaches. Even though the linguistics of parole is now better developed, it makes use of what the Croatian scholar Vladimir Ivir (1996:153) calls 'ad hoc catego-ries' that do not have "theoretical coherence and scientific rigour" because they are "not amenable to … theoretical treatment". The irony is that by the 1990s the whole idea of a scientific approach to translation had come under fire anyway.

The view that translation must be studied as parole (a communicative event) rather than langue (an abstract system) is now widely accepted, to the extent that an author like Pergnier (1993:223) can refer to it as a 'fact', and an important fact, since, as he says, it is because translation is a fact of parole that there is no such thing as the one 'right' translation of a message.

The langue/parole distinction is a very high-level distinction, concern-ing as it does the entire language. Saussure's other major distinction concerned one of the lowest levels of language, but was, if anything, even more revolu-tionary in its consequences.

Signifier/signified

If language is a structure, it must have component parts. The most important of these is the sign, a technical concept intended to get away from the
notion of 'word', which is notoriously difficult to define. The sign itself is a
structure that has two parts: the signifier and the signified, both of which are
mental states. The signifier is a mental image of the physical sound that you
make when you say, for example, *cat* or *koshka* (or *mimi* if you speak Tahi-
tian), while the signified is a mental concept or representation of physical
cats in the real world.

One of Saussure's key claims is that the link between the signifier and
the signified is not given by some Supreme Being or by Nature, as many
nonlinguists believe, but by society. The relation between the two is an arbitrary social construct. A tubular object consisting of meat and other
ingredients wrapped in a casing is assigned the signifier *sausage* in English
and *Wurst* in German. Neither of these is more 'right' than the other. There
is nothing magic in the object itself that makes *sausage* a 'better' word than
Wurst. It might seem that way, especially to people who speak only one
language, but in reality the link is purely arbitrary and no particular language has the 'right way' of saying things.

Perhaps one of the easiest ways to understand this is to consider the
phenomenon of political correctness. In a short space of time the supporters
of this ideology managed to create a whole new set of words to talk about
things for which they previously used the same words as everybody else.
They then tried, with varying success, to make their new words the social
norm. Altering an entire vocabulary in this way can only be possible because of the arbitrariness of the signifier-signified link.

Paradoxically, the same PC phenomenon demonstrates the deep-rooted
belief among many people that there *is* a special link between signifier and
signified. The attempt by some feminists to write the word *man* out of existence, even as a component of words where it has no connection with 'male
adult' (so that *emancipate* becomes *ewomancipate*), suggests a very strong
belief in word magic, in the power of the signifier to shape the way we think
about the signified. There is a joke about two farmers watching pigs wal-
lowing in the mud. After a time one says to the other, 'No wonder they be
called pigs'. This view is put with admirable succinctness by the comic
novelist Terry Pratchett (1989:132): "All things are defined by names. Change
the name, and you change the thing".

This kind of belief is not entirely irrational. If the signifier-signified
link is arbitrary, then translation would be very simple: you would identify
the signified, strip away the source-language signifier, and replace it with

the target-language signifier. According to this primitive theory of translation we would read the sign *sausage*, identify the language-independent signified denoted by the signifier, find its German signifier, and make a simple substitution: *sausage* would become *Wurst*. Translation would be a job for computers (a vast topic in itself which would be too technical for the present book to cover).

However, things are not that simple. Signs do not just signify (point to things in the real world). They also have value derived from language-internal structuring which is not the same from one language to the next. The words *cat* and *koshka* don't have the same range of meanings, so their value is different. English has two words *wood* and *forest* for the one Russian word *lies*, so again the values are different.

But words also carry a superstructure that is often referred to by the term 'connotation'. We think of some words as 'good' (*grandmother, baby, chocolate*) and other words as 'bad' (*spider, snot, slug*). But these connotational meanings are highly variable even within a language (some people don't like babies, others may have a fondness for spiders, while grandma may be the proverbial 'grandmother from hell') and they are often different between cultures. French people sitting down to eat remain calm in front of a plate of snails. Many English people would react differently, and so for them the menu may offer *escargots*, promising the exotic not the slimy. Connotation has proved difficult for linguistics to formalize, but we shall look at one useful attempt below.

Paradigmatic and syntagmatic: word sets and collocations

In addition to having its own internal structure, the sign can be structured in two other ways. Signs can be joined up in a string, and they can be grouped in a bundle. This is often called the 'chain and choice' model, and we shall see examples of how a translation problem that cannot be solved at one point in the chain may be solved by an appropriate choice at some other point. In the first case (making the chain) we produce word sequences: in the restaurant we can string words together to say 'I'd like sausage and chips, please'. The order in which we put the words is not normally random. It is governed by 'syntax', the rules of our language which tell us what kind of word can come in what place in a sentence. In another language we might have to say 'Like chipsausage would'. This is syntagmatic structure. Traditional linguistics handled syntax as a set of slots along the surface of the page or in the stream of spoken language; it tried to identify the function of each slot and what could go in it. Chomsky's revolution was to go below the surface and ask how the string was generated and from what.

In the second case (making the choice), we can pick words out of a 'bag' in place of other words. We could replace *sausage* in the above sentence by any number of words, such as *egg*, *pie* or *steak*. This is paradigmatic structure. But again the structure is not random. As we shall see below, words tend to group together to form semantic fields. Most people would associate *knives* with *forks* rather than with *cats and dogs* or any other non-cutlery items.

These groups may seem naturally ordered according to what is out there in the real world. But very often they, like the sign, are socially determined. Sticking with our food example, we find that the society we live in quite arbitrarily restricts what we are allowed to eat and in what combinations. *Tripe and chips* is not a combination found on English menus. Nor is *boiled potato and roast dog* or *broccoli and sautéd maggot*, although dogs and maggots are staple diet in other cultures, and this may pose problems for the translator. If we are translating a text in which the words *fish and chips* are chained together not to designate a particular combination of foods that somebody just happens to be eating but to convey the sociolinguistic connotation of 'typical national cheap meal', we may have to consider the possibility of some kind of cultural adaptation in our translation. This takes us outside linguistics, to a point where we can use linguistic concepts to describe the phenomena we find in language but where the guidelines on how to handle those phenomena in translation must come from some other discipline.

As the example of tripe and chips shows, the paradigmatic (picking items out of our lexical bag) and the syntagmatic (stringing them together in a line) come together in the concept of 'collocation', a technical term for what some people call a 'set phrase'. Except in special circumstances, such as poetry or madness, we can't take any old thing out of our language bag and stick it next to any other old thing. We are subjected to what are called 'selection restrictions'. These may be quite rigid (we say *bats in the belfry* not *bats in the steeple* to say that somebody is mad) or they may be quite loose: a British prime minister caused surprise with the phrase *two bananas short of a picnic* to mean the same thing, and although most English people say *egg and chips*, the heroine in the film *Shirley Valentine* called them *chips and egg*.

Some collocations are quite arbitrary. What possible link can there be between rain, cats, and dogs? And yet the English say *It's raining cats and dogs*. Others can be clearly motivated. The equivalent French expression *Il pleut comme vache qui pisse* ('It's raining like a cow urinating') is quite graphic. Good translation is often a case of either knowing or serendipitously hitting on the appropriate collocation (which will not always be in the dictionary).

Even people translating into their own language can get the collocation wrong, as happened with the student translator who produced the sentence *lost in a sea of explanations*, which is actually a mixing of two separate collocations (drowning in a sea / lost in a fog). Yet it should be said that collocations are not necessarily always right or wrong, but often simply more or less acceptable. You might get some idea of degrees of acceptability of collocation by asking yourself whether one can say *the cow strolled over to the fence*.

Because collocations are judged on a sliding scale of acceptability rather than just as right or wrong, not all speakers of a language agree on what is or is not a collocation. The Canadian theorists Jean-Paul Vinay and Jean Darbelnet (1958:89) give the translation pair *Échappe à l'analyse / baffles analysis*, which baffles quite a number of English people because they do not accept that *baffles analysis* is an English expression (maybe they've only ever heard 'defies analysis'). The fact that the dictionary definition of 'baffle' does not preclude it from collocating with 'analysis' does not, of course, mean that the collocation exists.

As Hans Hönig and Paul Kussmaul say (1984:98), diverging from the accepted collocations of the target language is not necessarily a bad thing to do, since there may be a good reason for it (poetry, for example). Yet where no good reason exists, such divergence thwarts reader expectation and causes a momentary disruption in text processing, producing what Ladmiral (1979:221) calls a braking effect on the ocular sweep of reading, an effect that will not have existed in the original. Note, though, that proponents of 'foreignizing translations', a concept we shall come back to, are entirely in favour of this braking process.

These concepts (sign, paradigm, collocation, etc.), together with others of a more traditional nature that we shall look at below, produced the structural linguistics which allowed a rigorous analysis of word and sentence structure.

Indeed, the chain-and-choice model was tremendously successful when applied to other areas of human experience that suddenly became readable as a form of language: selecting items from a semantic field (such as clothes) and chaining them together in socially constrained sequences that were really quite arbitrary (fashion). Such social construction is also found in two other branches of linguistics that are closer to a linguistics of parole than of langue, although they can still be analyzed in terms of the Saussurean concepts of signifier/signified and paradigm/syntagm. We shall introduce them briefly here, leaving greater detail to later chapters.

Sociolinguistics and pragmatics

The reference above to 'tripe and chips' can serve as a pointer to these other areas of linguistics. If I order 'tripe and chips' in a restaurant, the other customers may react in two ways: either I will be considered irredeemably vulgar, or I will cause a stir, or even both.

In the first case, I will have categorized myself as coming from a certain social class (there is little demand for tripe among the English middle classes) and possibly also as coming from a certain part of England (London or the North, perhaps), which may also be confirmed by my accent. This is the stuff of sociolinguistics, the study of language in relation to such things as age, class, regional origin and status. This is at the edge of linguistics because it shades over from language use into real-world knowledge and experience. Am I classified as lower class because of the words *tripe and chips* or because of the objects? The distinction is not always easy to make, and the Egyptian-born theorist Mona Baker (1992:183) goes so far as to say that it is "not particularly helpful" in the case of translation to try to distinguish the linguistic from the extralinguistic. However, since we must be careful not to overrate the role of linguistics in translation, we must try to make that distinction where possible.

If my demanding tripe and chips had been deliberately intended to create a stir, then we would be in another area of linguistics that goes under the name of pragmatics. This is defined as what it is we actually do with language, the things we accomplish by speaking and writing.

If, for example, I wish to show respect for somebody I am writing to, the way I accomplish that aim differs according to the language I use, and it would be absurd, except for specific purposes, to translate such formulae literally. Likewise, if I were translating a novel that contained the phrase *Can you lend me 100 yen*, I would not make a precise calculation from the current exchange rate. I would instead provide what has been called a set-to-set translation (Malone 1988:102), because what matters is not the precise sum but the act of asking for financial assistance.

By contrast, if I were translating an engineering document describing machine-tool parts and made the foolhardy decision to convert the measurements from metric to imperial, then it would become necessary to use a calculator because these figures are being put to a different use. (I have called this decision 'foolhardy' because one translator *did* make the conversion with catastrophic results: the manufactured parts were the wrong length by a margin that was minute but sufficient to render them useless. One thing linguistics will not tell translators is to make sure they have a good insurance policy to cover them against that kind of mistake.)

Before we move on to these wider areas of linguistics we need to come back to the concept of the sign, both as a structure within itself and as a structure with other units; we need to analyze its importance to translation.

2. Sub-Word Components

Sound

The clever trick about language lies in what has been called 'the double articulation'. Out of all the possible noises human beings can make (and which every baby makes in the first weeks of life), each language selects its own small number to produce a finite set of sounds specific to itself. This is the first articulation. In the second articulation the language then combines this finite set to form the potentially infinite set of words. That is the clever trick: a closed system that produces an open-ended system.

The study of sound belongs to a branch of linguistics called phonetics, which analyzes the sounds of a language using a highly technical terminology. In translation we mostly do not have to worry much about this level of language. However, in literary texts a lot of the time and in many other types of text some of the time, there are special sound effects such as alliteration (matching consonants, as in *make mine a Martini*) and assonance (matching vowels, as in *those lazy, hazy days of summer*) that can combine to special effect. Such effects can be described using the technical terminology of phonetics, but it isn't really necessary. We do not need to know that *make mine a Martini* makes use of an anterior voiced non-coronal bilabial nasal (m) alternating with an anterior voiced coronal unrilled nasal (n). Knowing the terminology is no use whatsoever if we read a text so rapidly or so carelessly that we don't even notice the sound effect in the first place. It is far more important for the translator to be sensitive to sound effects (some of which can be quite subtle), to judge to what extent the sound effect is intentional or accidental, and finally to assess the likelihood of its transfer to another language, although not necessarily using the same sounds.

A German text on illness tells us that half of the diseases that kill us come from what have *angefressen, angesoffen und angeschmokt* ('scoffed, guzzled, and smoked'), and the structural repetition would be hard to convey. In a French text about modern food production the author concludes that *nous l'avons standardisée, uniformisée, mondialisée. Donc, fragilisée.* Having noted the end rhyme (and some readers wouldn't) we need to ask if it is deliberate or simply pure chance that the words the author wanted to use just happened to have the same ending. Applying one of the rules of thumb devised by the American linguist Joseph Malone relating to the distance between the words involved (1988:205), we would have to say that the effect is almost certainly intended (we can never be 100% sure in a text of this kind) since the words come one after the other. But can the rhyme be translated? The first and third items can (*standardized, globalized*) but the

11

second and last are going to be a problem. How hard are we going to try to solve that problem?

The answer to this involves the 'minimax' concept, first applied to translation by the Czech translation theorist Jiří Levý (1967) and later pursued by the German Wolfram Wilss (1994). This principle says that people will strive to achieve maximum effect for minimum effort, and the amount of effort to be expended will be calculated according to each situation (of course, people may make the wrong calculation, spending too long on a problem they are not going to solve, or giving up too readily). In this particular case, since the main text function is to pass on information, a translator may think it not worth trying too hard (deadlines and the size of the translation fee will form part of the calculation), relying instead on serendipity or sudden insight to find 'homogenize' for the third element in the chain and despairing of solving the last one. This is another situation in which linguistics can help us define the problem and the terms of the solution, but where the end result will be influenced by factors external to linguistics.

The German author Rudolf Zimmer (1981) has examined a corpus of largely French-German literary translation over the centuries to see how translators deal with sound when it is used in wordplays. He finds a variety of responses to the problem, ranging from changing the device used (alliteration may become assonance), through various forms of explaining to the target-language reader that something has been lost in the translation, to full-blooded transposition in which the translator uses other words from the same or a similar semantic field that do not mean the same as the original but which do rhyme.

The most famous example of this approach is Levý's reference to the German poem *Ein Wiesel saß auf einem Kiesel inmitten Bachgeriesel* ('a weasel sat on a pebble in the middle of a babbling brook') in which the translator kept *weasel*, altering the rest of the poem to make it rhyme. Levý (1969:103-4) points out that the same effect could have been achieved by changing *weasel* to any other animal and altering all the other rhyming elements accordingly. In other words, only the most general meanings (an animal, a place to sit on, a place to sit in) need be translated.

The difficulty of achieving an adequate transfer of sound effects without extreme distortion of meaning is one reason why much rhymed verse is translated as blank verse nowadays, although a Spanish poet once deplored the reverse effect, complaining that "en ruso me riman" ("I get rhymed in Russian!") (personal communication).

Another area where the sound level may be important in translation is when a decision is taken to translate a text at the level of its sounds rather than its meaning. This situation is no doubt rare for most translators, yet it is also quite common in the sense that most languages can show examples. It involves making a paradigmatic choice of target-language words that sound as much as possible like those in the source language. The Russian word for 'Russian' (*ruskii*) might be translated as *rust key*, for example, or the German word for 'football' (*Fußball*) might be rendered as *fuzz ball*, neither of which has anything to with the original meaning. Left at this basic level, the result is likely to be nonsense and will give pleasure only to people who can appreciate the joke. If the decision is taken to make the words connect syntagmatically and semantically, it becomes possible to turn the source text into an entirely different target text that may or may not be on the same subject, so that we are playing a game of theme and variations over time. This is what the Zukofskys (1969) have famously done with the Latin poet Catullus.

Translating sounds is actually very difficult, but it can be fun to try. Take some famous phrase or advertising slogan, like *Vorsprung durch Technik*, and see what you can turn it into (the best I managed was *Boris pronged Dirk a nick*).

Sound translation may become the overriding concern in the dubbing of films. If the audience has a clear view of the mouth and lip movements of the characters, and there is a mismatch between what they see and what they hear, this can pose problems: the aesthetic effect may be destroyed, comprehension may be impaired, or it might quite simply be as irritating as an unscratchable itch. This is too complicated a topic to go into here (it will be dealt with in another book in the series), but dubbing can have unexpected side effects. In order to match the mouth movements for the English *I'm sorry*, German dubbers translate the phrase not with the usual equivalent of *Entschuldigung* but with *Es tut mir Leid* (to match the *m* sound), and this would now appear to be moving into the language of at least some Germans as a way of apologizing. The translation teacher Nigel Ross (1995) has described similar American influences on the Italian language also as a result of dubbing.

As we shall see in relation to the translation techniques of borrowing and calque, translation can have this effect of colonizing the target language with source-language structures and culture. Indeed, some translation theorists are now advocating the adoption of techniques to prevent such imperialism (see Douglas Robinson in this series). On a more mundane level, you might try to see for yourself just how difficult dubbing is by taking a famous line from a movie ('Frankly, my dear, I couldn't give a damn' from *Gone with the Wind*, for example) and trying to produce a dubbed version that will match the lip movements.

Translating sound may also be involved in the by no means negligible case when one wishes simply to transfer a foreign word or a proper name into the target text. Depending on the alphabet of the source-language, the words in question are translated alphabetically or by sound. An example will make the difference clear. When the Olympic games were held in Moscow, one of the BBC's sports reporters decided to give the viewers a spot of local colour by telling them about the language. Standing in front of a building with a sign, he said: "That may look like it's called a *pectopah*, but in fact it's a *restoran* or restaurant". In the first case he translated the letters; in the second he rendered the sound.

If a character in a French novel were called *Henri*, to change just one letter and translate him as *Henry* would be a move fraught with aesthetic, cultural and political problems. Consequently, the name would normally be transliterated alphabetically as *Henri*. But that gives people who don't speak French no idea of the sound, which is (roughly) *Onri*. Even if the sound mattered in some way, because the name is the subject of a pun such as *Henri, on rit* ('Henry, we're laughing'), the vast majority of translators would probably still rely on transliteration, perhaps overestimating the ability of their readers to pronounce a foreign language, and so not realizing the degree of loss in their translation.

If the source language uses an alphabet other than the Roman alphabet, however, then usually it is the sound which is translated. We translate the Russian name for *John* not as *Ibah* but as *Ivan*. Although even here, where you might imagine there was a prime case for international agreement, there is confusion in translation practice. The Russian genitive or 'possessive' case for masculine singular adjectives ends in *-ogo*, pronounced *-ovo*. Some publishers transliterate it alphabetically (*ruskogo*), while others transliterate it phonetically (*ruskovo*).

A famous example of sound being translated is found in Anthony Burgess's *A Clockwork Orange*, where Burgess used his own nontechnical system to create a kind of 'future slang' based on Russian, with words such as *horrorshow* for 'excellent' and *krovi* for 'blood', which will then have to be reproduced in some way in translation into other languages (presumably in Russian the effect is totally lost). Catford (1965:56-65) provides one of the few systematic, albeit very brief, discussions of translating sound and alphabet, a discussion that is perhaps not very useful for most of the trainee translators who read the book. However, in the field of anthropology, where the sounds and alphabets of unrecorded languages need to be studied, such matters come into their own.

Morphemes

At the level above individual sounds and letters, which are units without meaning, we find the morpheme, a word known only to academics until The Mighty Morphin Power Rangers brought it closer to the lives of the masses by their ability to change shape or 'morph' into mighty warriors. A morpheme (a shape unit) is defined as the lowest verbal unit which has meaning. If I say *cba*, I am producing an utterance that has no meaning in English (it doesn't even appear to be an acronym) and I would simply be producing a series of sounds for no apparent reason (I am unlikely to be spelling part of a word for somebody, since the *cb* combination is likely to be very rare, if it exists at all, in English). However, if I say *abc*, then I may well be producing a morpheme, as in *He doesn't even know the abc of the subject.* (Whether *abc* would actually be one morpheme or three is perhaps best left to people who enjoy such arguments.)

Translation at this level is a medium-to-rare phenomenon, and again one of its uses can be for literary entertainment. The famous 'Jabberwocky' poem by Lewis Carroll ('Twas bryllig and the slithy toves did gyre and gimble in the wabe …') is often assumed to be very difficult to translate because of its invented words made up of sounds and morphemes from other words (*slithy* from *lithe* and *slimy*). In fact, the individual parts of it ought to be quite easy to translate for precisely that reason. It is a fairly simple task to break an invented word like *bryllig* down into its morphemes (*bryll-* will be the root and *-ig* the adjectival ending), and it is then also a fairly simple task to find appropriate target-language morphemes (*bryllig* becomes *brilgeait* in French, for example), although getting the rhyme and the rhythm is a different matter altogether. Note how a morphemic analysis can demonstrate that grammar has meaning: *-ig* in *bryllig* may not have meaning in the same way that a word like *dog* has meaning, but it has the meaning of its grammatical function.

A more serious and more common form of morpheme transfer occurs in the translation of philosophical and scientific texts, where the translation technique called 'calque' (to be discussed below) enters into its own, albeit at a level lower than the one anticipated by Vinay and Darbelnet (1958), who gave us the term in this meaning. The English translators of the German philosopher Martin Heidegger frequently translate the morphemes of his compound words rather than try to invent a new English word, producing terms like *disclosedness* (for *Er-schlossen-heit*) that are not in any dictionary. New chemical substances or new technologies will often be translated morphemically into languages that do not readily use Greek and Latin as English and French do. In fact, even old chemical substances get this treatment. *Oxygen* means 'sour generating'. In German this has been translated more loosely as *Sauerstoff* ('sour stuff'), but in Russian it has been translated literally at the morphemic level as *kislorod*. Russian is a good example of how translation policy can constitute a language. A large number of even nonscientific Russian words are simply morphemic translations of Latin words into Russian roots. The word *soznaniye* ('conscience') is a literal translation into Russian of the Latin *con-* + *-scientia* ('with knowledge').

Finally, an interesting form of morphemic translation occurs quite frequently in translation practice without much note being taken of it, although it can often mean the difference between a good and a bad translation. In this case, rather than translating morpheme to morpheme, a practice that tends to be restricted to the areas listed above, we translate morpheme to word or phrase, a process that Catford called rank-shifted translation because we are going in this case from a unit at a lower rank, the morpheme, to a unit at a higher rank, the phrase. Two examples will show what is meant.

Languages differ in their willingness to pluralize nouns, and in such cases it can often be helpful to translate the source-language plural morpheme by lexical means, using a process that different translation theorists have all recognized but to which they have given different names ('dilution' and 'diffusion', for example). In this way, the plural morpheme of the source language becomes, in the target language, something like *the various forms of*, *the different categories of* and so on. Similarly, languages differ in their willingness to produce verbal nouns. Modern French seems quite happy to do this, and French writing on women's studies, for example, produces terms such as *infériorisation* or *minorisation*, where the morpheme *-isation* may have to be translated lexically in some languages by quite lengthy phrases such as 'the relegation of women to minority status'.

Many people writing in the tradition of deconstruction, post-structuralism and post-modernism have leant heavily for their terminology on the literal translation of French texts, and they have tended to reject the expansive translation technique I have just referred to, preferring instead to borrow or calque the term. This is presumably because producing a one-word expression (lexicalizing the term) gives it the dignity of an actually existing concept, bringing into being a word that can appear in the dictionaries of the future, whereas a diluted translation has the inferiority of a second-hand explanation and will never appear in any dictionary. In other words, we can spell out in linguistic terms what options are available in such translation situations, but the actual choice made will be guided by nonlinguistic considerations, political in this case. It is important for translators to be aware of these dimensions. (A less generous interpretation of cases like this, which are not new in translation, is that morphemically translating long foreign words is a way of disguising nonsense as high intellect.)

This concept of lexicalization is, by the way, one of the reasons why the French authorities have such difficulty in their never-ending attempts to eradicate English and American terms from their language: the French terms they propose are either not neatly lexicalized (they sound like explanations) or are composed of Greco-Latin roots that make them sound like scientific concepts rather than everyday items: calling a *radio tuner* a *syntoniser* not only gives a more technical term but also removes the cachet of using 'hip' language which is what young French people want.

Morphemic translation may sometimes be applied inappropriately. The Russian translation theorist Andrei Fedorov (1958:159) tells us that the German word *Rosenkranz* in a stage direction to the nineteenth-century German play *Maria Stuart* was broken down by the Russian translator into its component parts to give 'wreath of roses'. As a result, whenever the play was staged in Russia, Mary Queen of Scots turned up for her execution by decapitation sporting a jolly bunch of roses when she should have been carrying a rosary.

Componential analysis

To talk of morphemic translation is to recognize units of meaning smaller than the word, units that serve as building blocks to make words, just as sounds and letters are the building blocks for morphemes. The economic conditions of the 1980s produced a flurry of built-up words in English such as *downsizing*, *rightsizing* and *delayering*, which, in translation into many languages, may call for a diffusional translation technique when the concepts do not exist and cannot be packaged as individual words. The component parts are clear in these English words, but other words that seem not to be built up out of separate blocks in this way still turn out to be packages of meaning rather than one single meaning. Just as these words can be broken down phonetically into their component sound parts, so also they can be broken down semantically into their component meaning parts. This process has been called 'componential analysis' and one of its main protagonists (until recently) was Nida.

In componential analysis we use the notation [+meaning] and [-meaning] to represent the units of meaning that combine to make a word. The classic example given in the literature is: 'man' = [+adult] [+male] which at once shows the potentially ideological nature of the concept since women will ask why not: 'man' = [+adult] [-female]?

This kind of componential analysis is not usually of much use to a translator. To take another classic example, the fact that the French *mouton* can have the component [+animate] in its meaning of 'sheep' and [-animate]

17

in its meaning of 'mutton' is not going to give a seasoned or even semi-seasoned translator sleepless nights. This information may be fascinating to those whose speciality is the contrastive analysis of languages, but that is a different activity from translation. We saw the difference in our earlier example of the French *minorisation*, where we could list the semantic components and still be unsure as to whether we should translate it by an explanatory phrase or take the plunge and create the word 'minorization'.

Componential analysis at this level has been of use to translation firstly in anthropological linguistics, where it has served to compare and contrast such things as kinship structures and colour schemes in different cultures, and secondly in the translation of what are now called 'sensitive texts' such as the Bible. In the case of such texts some means must be found to transfer often difficult concepts into a culture in which they may seem very strange but where that strangeness must be overcome if the text is to have its effect. This process may involve the unpacking of the components into a phrase.

In most forms of day-to-day translation the problem of differing componential structure between languages usually disappears because of the context: only the novice translator is likely to confuse the German *Fleisch* meaning 'meat' [-human] and the same word when it means 'flesh' [+human], a pretty important distinction in cooking but not a serious translation problem. However, the English translators of the French television soap opera *Châteauvallon* did not take componential structure into account when they translated *un garçon de trente ans* as *a thirty year old boy* rather than *a thirty year old bachelor*. In the context ('a thirty year old *garçon* doesn't live with his parents, he has his own place'), *garçon* was probably marked [-married] rather than [-adult], hence bachelor.

Many of the cases covered in studies of componential analysis are far less interesting from our point of view, although immensely important for language learners. They concern the kind of vocabulary and meaning distinctions that form part of foreign-language competence rather than translator competence, whereas the problem with *garçon* does concern translator competence, because it involves a nexus of knowledge about word meaning, cultural usage, context, and the capacity for textual interpretation. One of the main uses of componential analysis is not with single words but with series of words, which we shall look at under the heading of semantic sets.

3. Semantics

In moving from the level of sound to the level of morphemes and word components, we have moved into the area of linguistics called semantics, which is the study of meaning.

The disenchantment of translation theorists and practitioners with linguistics is often said to arise from the initial refusal of structural linguistics to address the question of meaning on the grounds that it was scarcely structured and, in any case, located in the 'black box' of the mind where it was unobservable and so unavailable to scientific study. A classic textbook of the time, Charles Hockett's *A Course in Modern Linguistics* (1958), has no chapter on meaning. However, a linguistics that ignores meaning is not much use to translation studies, for which the question of meaning is absolutely central. As Catford says, "It is clearly necessary for translation-theory to draw upon a theory of meaning" (1965:35).

Linguistics fairly quickly came to the task of modelling meaning both at word and sentence level. At word level it produced concepts we have already referred to or will consider below, such as denotation, connotation, componential analysis and semantic fields. On the level of sentence meaning, it has developed concepts such as presupposition and entailment, which will only partly concern the translator.

Semantic fields

The importance of these concepts for translation is that their application in comparative linguistics demonstrates clearly that meanings and meaning structures do not match between languages. From a linguistic point of view, one could say that each language is full of gaps and shifts when compared with other languages. Just as butchers in one country take the same animal and cut it up in different ways from butchers in another country, so languages take what is apparently the same external reality and slice it differently. Another view says that languages actually create 'external reality', which may or may not be there, but that is a philosophical question beyond the scope of this book.

One of the most spectacular and frequently quoted examples of the differential slicing of reality is supposed to be the ability of the Inuit to name many more different types of snow than other people (a feature put to some use in the novel *Miss Smilla's Feeling for Snow*). But there are more homely examples. Most English speakers will normally use just the one word to refer to their home lighting ('Put the light on'), whereas some French people may slice things up differently and refer to them by a number of different terms relating to the shape or position: I knew a French family which used *anneau* for a circular neon light in the kitchen and *rapplique* for a wall-fitted light in the sitting room. In other words, in the semantic field of 'house lighting', just as in other semantic fields (gardening terms, literary genres, furniture ..., the list is endless), different languages will have a different number of terms in different relationships to one another.

This affects not just things but actions as well. Carl James (1980:93), for example, has contrasted the English terms for 'cook' with the much more restricted number of German terms where the word *kochen* has to stand in for *cook*, *boil* and *simmer*, and where, in spite of all the odds apparently stacked against them, Germans still manage to avoid food poisoning. This is where componential analysis comes in handy for marking out the distinctions, although the terms we are about to use will hopefully be more fruitful for translators.

In the lighting example, the English use what is called a 'hypernym' (a more general term) while the French use a series of 'hyponyms' (more specific terms); in the cooking example it is English which has the hyponyms and German the hypernyms. These terms turn out to be important for translation: just as we saw above that differences in componential structure may call for special translation techniques of repackaging, so in the realm of semantic fields the interplay between hypernym and hyponym turns out to offer a useful technique for solving translation problems. A very simple example occurs for those translating between English and Russian where the English hyponyms *arm* / *hand* and *leg* / *foot* conflate into the Russian hypernyms *ruka* and *noga* respectively. (When Russians go to their doctor with a pain in their *noga*, they have to use different words again to make clear which part is hurting.) A comparable phenomenon is found in the strange case quoted by Igor Mel'cuk (1978:292) of a language that has no word for 'foreskin', only two hyponyms, one meaning 'uncircumcized male member' and the other meaning 'circumcized male member'. In the translation of the Biblical command to 'Bring back the foreskins of the Philistines' rather more got chopped off than was intended.

This phenomenon of slicing the world up differently occurs within languages as well as between them. The French scholar Georges Mounin, one of the earliest linguistic commentators on translation, gives examples from the semantic field of French bread (1963:65). Now, I was at pains in the previous paragraph to say that only some French people use different terms for their lighting, and the same is true of Mounin's bread: not all of them are used by all French people. In England, too, words such as *bap*, *bun* and *teacake* will either not be used by all English people or will not refer to the same objects in different parts of the country. Languages differ in the number of hyponyms at their disposal and whether or not there are hypernymous terms in a particular field. These gaps create problems in translation.

It may also be the case that one language just doesn't make use of the possibilities available to it in the same way as another language. Vinay and Darbelnet (1958:60) point to the apparent paucity in French of a semantic field expressing sound. French, they claim, can only say 'un bruit de soie, de chaises' ('the *noise* of silk or of chairs') whereas English can say 'the *rustle* of silk, the *scraping* of chairs'. Yet as André Malblanc (1963:46) points out, French does have a quite rich semantic field in this area of meaning but seems more reluctant to use it (the reason given by Malblanc is that the words are 'heavy', although the real reason lies in the attempts made in the seventeenth and eighteenth centuries to purge the vocabulary for literary purposes).

Even where words seem to have an unproblematic match between two languages in a given semantic field, this often turns out not to be so. In claiming above that *sausage* and *Wurst* denote the same object, I deliberately ignored the many differences between them: what they are made of, what they are eaten with, how they are cooked, and so on. Similarly, Italian butter and English butter would also seem superficially to occupy the same place in the field of foodstuffs, but the English academic Susan Bassnett (1980:18) has shown they are not really the same thing: the composition and colour are different, they are used differently in the preparation of meals, and they have different social status. Nonetheless, one would usually want to translate the Italian word *burro* by the English word *butter*, the German word *Wurst* by the English word *sausage* and accept the loss of the noncentral meanings. This is the sort of loss that makes some people declare translation to be an impossible undertaking, a view which ignores the fact that there are also gains in translation.

Word relations

Words enter into relations other than that of general-specific, and you will find these dealt with in detail in the standard works on semantics. The English linguist Geoffrey Leech (1981), for example, discusses synonymy (words with the same meaning), polysemy (words with several meanings), and homonymy (words which look or sound alike but which have different meanings), and breaks down antonymy (words with opposite meanings) into several classes:

• binary taxonomic oppositions (alive/dead), where two opposite terms describe all possibilities for a particular field of meaning, although we can add other terms to produce a gradient ('He was more dead than alive');

- multiple taxonomic oppositions (single/married/divorced), the semantic fields discussed earlier;
- polar oppositions (large/small), which work on a scale rather than as straight opposites (some quite large people feel quite small when they discover they are sharing their living space with a spider or a mouse);
- relative oppositions (up/down), which involve a directional vector, in other words they point in different directions from one another, as in 'I own this/This belongs to me'.

Like so many other linguistic terms, few of these concepts are unproblematic from the theoretical point of view. Yet our concern here is not to get involved in problems of definition but rather to establish whether or not the concepts are useful for translators. If I am adamant that I do not need to know that an unvoiced pharyngeal spirant is what gives the alliteration in 'happy hour' (that time in English pubs when the drink is cheap), could I equally adamantly agree with Albrecht (1973:47) when he says that the concept of synonymy is "only of marginal importance" for translation? The answer is a qualified no. Qualified, because we need, as always, to distinguish between the usefulness of these terms in acquiring foreign language competence and their applicability to the translation process. But the distinction is not always an easy one to make in this area.

Knowing that the Russian word *dubio* is a polyseme (meaning either 'cudgel' or 'blockhead') or that the German word *Hals* is a homophone (two words with the same sound but different meanings) is knowledge to be acquired when learning the language, a matter of language competence. However, when the translator of a travel brochure writes the phrase 'If you enjoy idleness', we are dealing with two types of competence: language (in)competence, since the translator has not learnt the negative meaning of 'idleness' as opposed to the more positive 'lazing about', and translation competence, since the translator has not learnt to apply such translation concepts as text type, text function and verbal routines (a native speaker writing a travel brochure would have produced the more appropriate phrase 'If you just want to relax in the sun'). The same travel brochure also told its readers 'thus you will remain lying on rocks or on pebbles getting sunburnt', which is not calculated to cause a stampede to the airport.

In the case of the 'directional vectors' mentioned above, Malone (1988:85) is able to show that there can be good translation reasons for replacing a source-language phrase like 'That pleases me' with a target-language phrase like 'I like that'. The reasons might be on the level of style (one is more formal than the other) or information flow (the preceding part of the translation may have been written in such a way that we are now obliged to begin with 'I'), or formal parallelism of structures to produce some textual effect.

Similarly, there may often be good reasons for choosing a synonym rather than the obvious translation of an SL item (variety, euphony, formality level might be some such reasons), and the use of polar opposites in a restructured sentence is a frequent translation device, as we shall see in the section on translation techniques.

The problem with our example of *idleness* versus *relaxation* is that even on holiday many people do not like to think of themselves as 'idle'. Being idle is a bad thing; being relaxed is good. The words have different connotational meanings.

Connotation

"This is not a very useful term", says Palmer (1981:92), the author of a standard English book on semantics. And yet Ladmiral devotes over 100 pages to the topic (1979:115-246). Leech (1981:12) discusses connotative meaning as just one aspect of associative meaning, all those elements of meaning that attach in some way to a word without being a 'real' or central part of its meaning and which can vary enormously from person to person or culture to culture. Where one culture sees a fluffy pet, another culture sees a food item or a pavement soiler; where one culture sees stinking excrement, another culture sees a substance with medicinal properties. One can begin to understand Palmer's reluctance to entertain the notion.

Take the French word *brioche*. The dictionary translates this as *brioche (a sort of bun)*, meaning that there is no apparent equivalent for this object in English even at the denotational level. That being so, how is one to translate the connotational dimensions of the word? A sentence like *On va manger de la brioche* will be uttered with relish by many French people because it is a treat (although unappreciative foreigners like myself find it not at all sweet and rather dry to eat). It is also served for the Fête des Rois (Twelfth Night) when it contains plastic figurines representing the king and the queen (it used to be beans, but that's progress), and those who find them in their piece of *brioche* get to wear paper crowns. It was also the word Marie-Antoinette used in her famous declaration *Let them eat cake*, when she was told the populace were revolting because they had no bread to eat. This shows just how difficult the word is to translate since *brioche* lies somewhere between bread and cake and poor old Marie-Antoinette was not being quite as heartless as the English translation makes her seem.

Similarly, in my Chamber's English dictionary, I find 'Cantal: a hard, full-fat French cheese made from cow's milk, from the *Cantal* department of the Auvergne'. As a definition of the denotational meaning, that's fine. But to French people it's just one of a wide choice of cheeses (paradigmatic) to accompany various other foods and drinks (syntagmatic) and will evoke memories of texture, taste and smell, possibly repugnance for non-cheese eaters, and beyond that there lie memories of geography and culture (the Auvergnats, living in the centre of France, have their own special place in the folklore of everyday life: they are stubborn, they pronounce -s- as -sh-, they work hard, many of them became café owners in Paris …).

Faced with this load of connotational meaning, how is a translator to cope without lapsing into lengthy commentary? Here again we are at the limits of how much linguistics can contribute to translation, since nothing in linguistics itself will actually help us solve this particular problem. But what linguistics can do for us is give us some help in defining the problem.

Clearly, the range of information I provided for *brioche* and *cantal* is so wide and so disparate that some way must be found to portion it out and deal with it more systematically rather than lumping it all under one heading. One of the few, and often criticized, attempts to deal with connotational meaning in a systematic way comes from Osgood, Succi and Tannenbaum (1957). The details of their work and the criticisms of it need not be repeated here. In practice, translators have to work with connotation whether or not theoretical linguists are happy with the term. As Ladmiral says, "Translatology cannot be content with applying linguistic theory; it has to manage a practice, day by day; it is a praxeology" (1979:162).

The research conducted by Osgood, Succi and Tannenbaum led them to the conclusion that speakers react to words in three dimensions: words are good or bad, active or passive, strong or weak. The Edinburgh-based scholars Basil Hatim and Ian Mason (1990a:114) give the example of *Islamic fundamentalists* and the different 'connotations' the term would have in Western and Islamic media. The 'connotational' meanings they list are in fact examples of associational meaning, which are potentially unlimited: in the Western media Islamic fundamentalists are associated with fanaticism, terrorism and so on, while in Islamic media they are associated with martyrdom and sacrifice. The connotational meanings in the terminology of Osgood and company are much more restricted: in this case the Western connotations would be active, strong but bad, while the Islamic connotations would be active, strong and good. In our earlier case of *brioche* the major connotational component would be 'good' (but not for me).

The French academics Hélène Chuquet and Michel Paillard (1987:220), who restrict their brief discussion to the positive/negative axis, indicate the kinds of pitfalls that arise from connotational meaning. A neophyte translator from French to English might see no problem in translating the French *juvénile* as English *juvenile* without bothering to check the dictionary. Yet the nontechnical usage of the word tends to be positive in French and negative in English (calling somebody *juvenile* is quite an insult). This emerges only indirectly from the dictionary, which gives *young, youthful* as translations of the French *juvénile*. You have to notice that *juvenile* is not there and ask yourself why not in order to realize there is a problem.

Although this view of connotational meaning is more limited than, for example, Leech's description of the phenomenon, it is easier to grasp. It might have helped the student translator who unthinkingly produced the translation *dreadful adventures*, which, for no good reason, links a 'bad' word (*dreadful*) with a 'good' word (*adventures*), a negative with a positive, and so sets up a slight conflict in the reader's mind. This phenomenon demonstrates that it is not enough to get connotation right for the individual word; one must take account of higher units. In a text on the likelihood of the Holocaust ever being repeated, for example, the student translator who wrote of a *repeat performance* might have decided, on consideration of connotational meaning, that the term was inappropriate to the subject matter.

However we account for it, the fact remains that connotational meaning is difficult to translate. Indeed, such difficulties raise the question of the fundamental impossibility of good translation of anything other than technical texts. Ladmiral's solution is to propose a series of translation techniques, not all of which he explains very satisfactorily, ranging from nontranslation, where the translator deems the connotational meaning to be unimportant, via 'periparaphrase' (1979:219), which builds some form of explanation into the text, to 'minimal mistranslation' (ibid:244), where the connotation of a word is deemed more important than its denotation. As an example of the latter he refers to Nida and Taber's discussion of the Greek word *gunai* in the New Testament, translated denotatively as *woman* in the King James Bible but connotatively as *mother* in the New English Bible to mark the word positively (showing affection and respect). Yet this kind of approach may ultimately lead to much-maligned examples like translating the Biblical *Lamb of God* by *Seal of God* for Inuit readers. Before crossing this line into the risky territory of cultural adaptation, most translators will want to test other techniques, perhaps of the kind examined below.

Word meaning and translation

The variation between languages in the different components and relations of word meaning has two consequences for translation. Firstly the meaning that is transferred will be decided by situation and context, not by the dictionary, and secondly, the transfer will nearly always involve some form of loss or change. These are both now a commonplace of linguistic theories of translation. As Catford (1965:49) says, "The SL [source-language] and TL [target-language] items rarely have the same 'meaning' in the linguistic sense; but they can function in the same situation", while Albrecht (1973:23) tells us that human translation "is always to some extent 'false'".

The same Albrecht (1973:5) uses the interesting analogy of currency transfer: although the aspect and numerical value of the coins and notes change, their 'real' value should not, but in reality it does, since they fit into a different price structure. He could also have said that they fit into a cultural system with different purchasing priorities. He points to the considerable differences in 'pure' meaning between the French *je suis allée à la gare pour chercher mon frère et ma sœur* and the German *ich bin zum Bahnhof gefahren um meine Geschwister abzuholen* (1973:10). The two most obvious differences are that the French shows the speaker to be a woman whereas the German doesn't, and the German tells us the speaker used motorized transport whereas the French doesn't. Another difference is that German can package *brother and sister* into one item. Yet none of this prevents the two sentences from being perfectly adequate situational translations of one another.

The second consequence of meaning differences between languages is that one task of a linguistic theory of translation becomes that of defining the catalogue of translation techniques required to overcome these mismatches. The literature is quite full of such catalogues, or taxonomies. In the next chapter we shall look at three: the most famous from Vinay and Darbelnet, and work done by two Russian scholars and one American expert.

4. Translation Techniques

Russian approaches

The Russian translation theorist Yakob Retsker (1974:9) describes three types of relationship between a source language and a target language:

i   equivalence;
ii   variant and contextual correspondence;
iii all other types of translational transformation.

The changing terminology is intended to alert us to a fundamental difference between equivalence and the two other categories based on the langue/parole distinction. For Retsker, equivalence is a fact of langue: a one-to-one relationship between the source language and target language term regardless of context. One would thus expect a term like *carbon monoxide* to be translated the same way at all times into whatever the target language. This would come under the study of terminology, where the one-to-one relationship between name and thing would theoretically allow us to implement a 'primitive' translation theory of word-for-word substitution. Such a theory is expressed in Jumpelt's declaration (1961:57) that the translator's task is "to produce relations between the TL [target-language] unit and O [object] which largely correspond to the relations between the SL [source-language] unit and O". In the scientific and technical literature that Jumpelt is talking about you would expect this strategy to succeed, although even in that kind of literature there are many factors that make the task harder than it might seem.

   Retsker's two other categories of correspondence and transformation, which his compatriot Shveitser renames 'analogy' and 'adequacy' (1987:25), are facts of parole, where the translation will be dependent on factors such as context and text function.

Translation as 'analogy'

Analogy covers the situation of one-to-many correspondences between languages. This is the usual case as we saw in our introductory discussion of meaning. Opening a Spanish-English dictionary at random I find, on the same page, the one-to-one equivalence of the technical term *nefritis / nephritis*, and the one-to-several correspondence of *necesidad* meaning *necessity, need, tight spot, poverty* and *business* (as a euphemism for *excrement*). Retsker quotes the Russian dictionary as giving no fewer than eight translations of the English word *sincere* (1974:14). The German dictionary gives six translations, but the French dictionary only three. In other words, how we translate this word will vary according to the microcontext and will be subject to selection restrictions. In some cases the context will reduce the solutions available to just one-to-one equivalence. If the microcontext is *friend* then our choice in Russian reduces to one word because the collocation is fixed.

Dictionaries have become increasingly helpful in this respect but they cannot be trusted entirely. My Spanish dictionary gives just one translation for *sincere*. Is this because English *sincere* and Spanish *sincero* are pancontextual equivalents whereas in German, French and Russian we have only contextual correspondences? Or is it because the makers of the Spanish dictionary have decided to save some space on this word? Only translators who have built up their own internal dictionary (or those with a better dictionary than mine) will know the answer.

Even where a dictionary provides contextual help, it can be misleading. Students translating a text on the Holocaust which referred to *la déportation des Juifs* found under *déportation* in the dictionary '(*internement*) imprisonment (in a concentration camp)'. Given such precise information, they thought they were dealing with an equivalent and wrote either *imprisonment* or *internment*, but in fact we are dealing here with a contextual variational correspondence: the context (the subject matter in this case) requires *deportation*. The term *imprisonment* would be neutral, while the word *internment* would have associational meanings that would be different for different groups of people (Japanese-Americans might remember their internment in World War II, while older British people would associate the term with Northern Ireland). The possibility of causing offence by mistranslating such terms is great, which demonstrates the need for translators to have encyclopaedic knowledge extending way beyond the purely linguistic.

The dictionary can also be misleading in what would seem to be very clear-cut cases of equivalence. I quoted above the randomly selected case of *nefritis* translated only as *nephritis* in the dictionary. But there are many situations in which one would want to translate it as *inflammation of the kidneys*, just as one might wish to translate the French *infarctus du myocarde* by *heart attack* rather than *myocardial infarction*. It is this latitude even in the handling of apparently straightforward equivalences which leads people like Jean Delisle and Marianne Lederer to reject the narrowly linguistic categorizing of theorists such as Retsker in favour of what they call the 'interpretative' approach.

Translation as 'adequacy'

Retsker's final category, which he calls 'all other translational transformations' and which Shveitser calls 'adequacy', covers cases where there is no one-to-one equivalence and no readily definable contextual correspondence in the form of a collocation. In these cases the translator departs from the wording of the original, and from the dictionary offerings, to use one of four translation techniques. Retsker (1974:39) actually lists seven, but we shall follow Shveitser (1973:25-28), who does some reorganizing.

1. Concretization

Related to our earlier discussion of hyponymic/hypernymic shifts in translation are what Retsker calls 'concretization' or 'differentiation', with its corollary 'generalization'. The German *Geschwister*, for example, could be translated as the more concrete and differentiated *brothers and sisters* or as the more abstract and undifferentiated *siblings*, depending on context and desired effect. An example taken at random from French might be the abstract *fumerolle* which, according to context, we can translate either by the technical term *fumarole* or by the concrete and differentiated *volcanic smoke and gas,* while German offers examples such as *Mußheirat* (a 'must-wedding') which could be translated either as an equally abstract *forced wedding* or as the very concrete *shotgun wedding.*

Another example from French would be the translation of the already concrete *charentaises* by the double concrete *pipe and slippers* in an attempt to convey the associational and connotational meaning of a certain kind of conservative, conformist, stay-at-home man, even though such a translation would be culturally problematic, since the Frenchman in question would be more likely to smoke a Gauloise cigarette than a pipe.

In all of these cases, linguistics can explain what is going on (abstract-concrete switching) but cannot necessarily tell us what solution to adopt, since the criteria for that would depend on a wide variety of factors such as world knowledge, reader expectation, information loading, text type, desired effect, and even the politics of translation.

Retsker gives the apparently straightforward example *Have you had your meal?* where the generic *meal* must become the more precise *break-fast/dinner/supper* in translation into Russian. But even here we need sociolinguistic and world knowledge, since "for an English person from a well-to-do bourgeois family, dinner-time almost coincides with supper-time for a working-class family" (Retsker 1974:42).

A less straightforward example given by Retsker (1974:41) is the word *ruthless* in the text *ruthless newspaper jingoism*, where he claims the term is being used not in its normal meaning of 'without mercy' but simply as an intensifier, so that it can be translated into another language by a generalized term such as 'unrestrained'. The most likely candidate in a language such as French would be *acharné*, which is not given in the dictionary under *ruthless*, where we find only what Retsker would call true equivalents meaning 'without mercy'.

If the word we need is not in the dictionary, will reference to Retsker's taxonomy help us find it? The answer is, of course, no, not directly. Does this mean the taxonomy is useless? We shall come back to this question in general terms below, but an immediate answer in reference to this particular example is that application of the taxonomy would have stopped us looking in the wrong place in the dictionary to begin with. Realizing that the word *ruthless* was being used here not in its precise concrete meaning but as a generalized negative intensifier should have triggered a search for contextual variants in English, sending us to the monolingual synonym dictionary as a first step, and from there to the right place in the bilingual dictionary.

2. Logical derivation

The English expression *shorter working hours* expresses the result or effect of an action (hours have become shorter as a result of some action taken), whereas the German and French equivalents – *Senkung der Arbeitszeit* and *réduction de la semaine de travail* (reduction in work time/ working week) – express the cause. The relation between the English on the one hand and the French and German on the other is one of logical modulation. Retsker's illustration of this translation technique (1974:45) is *acid test*: the English term refers to a process whereas one possible Russian translation ('litmus paper') refers to the object used in the test.

If actions are complexes consisting of 'cause-process-effect', then the source language may express an action by focusing on one of these elements, while the target language focuses on another. This is a form of the literary device known as metonymy: if we say *With one thrust of his trusty blade, Dirk was free*, we are using the part (blade) to express the whole (knife or sword). An interlingual example would be *to go for a sail* (part) / *ir de paseo en barco* (whole) (Vázquez-Ayora 1977:297). Shveitser says (1987:30) this kind of metonymic transfer is very frequent in translation, and indeed it forms the basis of another famous translation taxonomy provided by Vinay and Darbelnet, to which we shall come shortly. Douglas Robinson (1991), an ardent opponent of a strictly linguistic approach to translation, even sees it as a translation strategy in itself.

Different languages achieve this kind of correspondence in different ways. The French for *acid test* involves no logical derivation but simply a generalization (*épreuve décisive*), while the German term *Feuerprobe* ('test by fire') involves a different semantic domain.

The examples we have given of this particular translation technique would not seem to be very productive. Translators who don't know how to translate *acid test* will turn to a dictionary not to a taxonomy. However, the word they want may not be there (my Spanish dictionary offers nothing), while over-reliance on dictionaries can be time-consuming and lead to poor translations, so a professional translator might achieve better results by thinking taxonomically and going straight to a generalizing translation. This would be true of *renoncer* in the phrase *les Européens doivent renoncer à la facilité* where time spent consulting the dictionary would be time wasted since none of the translations given are satisfactory (*give up* is too colloquial, *renounce* too formal and collocationally restricted, *relinquish* and *abandon* are the wrong meaning). It would be far better to look for logical connections that might supply a more appropriate translation. The usefulness of a taxonomy is not in supplying ready-made solutions to a particular problem so much as suggesting general problem-solving methods.

3. Antonymic translation

Antonymic translation is translation by the opposite. It is frequently used to achieve what is felt to be a more natural wording in the target language. Thus the French *est une valeur déjà ancienne* may be translated literally (*is an already old value*) but could also be translated as *is by no means a new value*. Retsker (1974:48-9) gives examples such as *The woman at the other end asked him to hang on* translated into Russian as *not to hang up the phone* and *wrote with perseverance* as *worked without a break* for reasons of 'naturalness'. There are many translation situations where this technique can be useful.

4. Compensation

Compensation is a technique used by some translators (others reject it) when something in the source language is not translatable. The term covers so many situations that there is a danger, according to Shveitser (1987:32), echoing Vinay and Darbelnet (1958:189), of seeing all translation as compensation and of overzealous translators turning their task into one of comment or even total adaptation and rewriting.

Vinay and Darbelnet devote some four pages to the concept, which they see as the making good in one part of the text of something that could not be translated in another (1958:189). Vázquez-Ayora, whose book is a development of their work into Spanish, devotes ten whole pages to the subject

(1977:373-384). Jiří Levý (1969:58) views compensation more as an element of langue and takes the sunny view that where a linguistic subsystem is richly developed in one language but absent or poorly developed in another, the second language will have other systems to compensate, as with the Russian aspectual system that compensates for a limited tense system.

One frequently cited situation requiring compensation is the translation of dialects. We shall say no more about the issue here, since it will come up again in our section on sociolinguistics. Instead, let us take as our first example a case quoted by Retsker (1974:53) in which a character in a Galsworthy novel alters the sum on a cheque from *nine* to *ninety* pounds simply by adding two letters. Since the Russian word for 'nine' (which ends in -*at*) cannot easily be altered to the word for 'ninety' (which ends in -*nosto*) the Russian translator has been forced to compensate by reducing the sums to 'eight' and 'eighty'. Retsker makes the point that in French the forger would have to be even more modest (only 'five' and 'fifty' lend themselves to the manoeuvre), which begs the question whether there might not be some languages in the world where the sum would be either so small as to make the game not worth the candle, or so astronomical as to make the forgery self-denouncing.

However, although Retsker makes the point that changing French *cinq* ('five') to *cinquante* ('fifty') requires five extra letters (as does the Russian 'eight' to 'eighty' conversion), he overlooks the fact that in real life there is unlikely to be sufficient space on a cheque to insert all those extra letters. A problem that is linguistically definable (converting a number by morphemic addition) and linguistically solvable (trawl the number system for a compensatory substitute) turns out in practice to be fraught with real-world restrictions.

Although this example has a reality problem, it is nonetheless clearly a situation where compensation is called for, and one must applaud the translator for being sufficiently eagle-eyed to notice there was a problem (many would not). The two areas of compensation discussed by Vinay and Darbelnet (1958:189-191) also seem unproblematic. The first concerns the fact that in many languages the words for 'you' depend on the degree of familiarity between the people speaking. The second area of compensation, which we shall deal with in the discussion of sentence structure, concerns the fact that some languages use linguistic devices for emphasis that are not available in other languages. Clearly, some form of compensation is required in these cases to avoid translation loss.

The first case (forms of address) is widely discussed in the literature, so I shall simply mention here two rather unusual examples of it. In the film *Man Bites Dog* (the imaginative translation of the original Belgian *C'est arrivé près de chez vous*), a serial killer is having dinner with his friends (it can happen). In a sudden fit of rage he shoots one of them dead, whereupon a woman who had been using the familiar *tu* prudently switches to the more respectful *vous*, a switch that the killer comments upon. The subtitler compensated for the absence of an equivalent by using the word *Sir*, a frequent but not always plausible solution.

The second example comes from *Miss Smilla's Feeling for Snow* (Høeg 1993:239), which handles the situation rather differently, giving the following rather odd exchange of dialogue:

> "What's your native language?"[1]
> "You mean, what's *your* native language", he corrects me gently, substituting the formal form of address.

where the not very visible footnote number (even less visible because unexpected in a novel) directs the reader to a linguistic explanation at the bottom of the page.

Vinay and Darbelnet restrict the scope of compensation to adjacent text areas: the compensatory feature will be found within a few words of the segment in which there was a problem, as in our two examples. Where compensation becomes unsavoury to many translators is in the suggestion that it can be used to maintain a more global textual balance.

One of the greatest difficulties in translation is wordplay. If the subject of a text forces the translator to remain within the same semantic domain as the pun, and if the target language quite simply has no two words in that domain that can form a wordplay, then the pun is untranslatable. How, for example, are we to translate the pun in *le socialisme français est un cadavre exquis* where the last two words can be taken quite literally as 'good-looking corpse' (socialism was dead), but also as a reference to the Surrealist game of Consequences (French socialism was a jumble of disparate tendencies). There would seem to be no possibility of translating this wordplay.

The suggestion made by some is that a translator should compensate for such a loss by producing a pun in some other part of the text where none exists in the original. One proponent of this kind of strategy is the German translation theorist Güttinger (1963:75), quoted approvingly by Zimmer who calls it "a perfectly useful suggestion" (1981:53). Many translators find this quite repugnant, however, and one's reaction to the idea is likely to depend on wider, non-linguistic issues such as the prevalent ideological atmosphere, publisher practice and copyright laws.

The view from Canada

Retsker and Shveitser's taxonomies are only two of quite a large number of attempts to formalize the procedures involved in translation. The most famous, and one of the most criticized, is undoubtedly the one proposed by Vinay and Darbelnet in 1958.

These two authors base their theory of translation on two elements. Firstly, they use the apparatus of Saussurean linguistics: langue/parole, signifier/signified, the structuring of language at the level of grammar, lexis and what they call the 'message', the textual and situational level. Secondly, they make use of the notion that each language has its own 'spirit' which systematically compels it to express itself in one way rather than another. This latter element has been disparaged by later commentators. Albrecht talks of the "sinister proximity of folk-psychological tracts" (1973:74) while Chuquet and Paillard warn against "hasty generalisations of folk psychology" (1987:32). Presumably, however, a more sophisticated form of this concept informs the 'foreignizing' strand in translation theory that warns against colonization and enslavement of the Other produced precisely by using some of the translation techniques advocated by Vinay and Darbelnet.

These translation techniques, which we look at next, are 'borrowing', 'calque', 'literal translation', 'transposition', 'modulation', 'equivalence' and 'adaptation', each of which can be applied at the linguistic levels of lexis, grammar and text.

Borrowing

The source-language form is taken into the target language, usually because the latter has a gap in its lexicon, although the technique can be used for other reasons. When the Russians launched the first space satellite, the Western press borrowed the term *sputnik* until we learned to call them *satellites*. But the terms *glasnost* and *perestroika* describing policies pursued by the former Soviet leader Gorbachov continue to be used as borrowings for their exotic flavour, "to create a stylistic effect", as Vinay and Darbelnet would say (1958:47), when they could actually have been translated quite simply as *openness* and *reconstruction*.

Borrowing a term when a possible translation exists might be intended, as Fedorov says (1953:160-61), to retain the "shade of specificity" in the foreign object or institution, perhaps adding the translation or some form of explanation to assist the reader. Other reasons may be to convey a sound effect or to ensure that a cultural Other is not translated entirely out of existence.

One often overlooked area of borrowing is in the domain of brand names, where problems of sound and meaning can arise. A story commonly told in translation circles is that the makers of the deodorant *Bodymist* launched the product onto the German market under the same name because nobody told them that in German *Mist* means 'manure'. Deciding whether to borrow, translate or adapt a product name into a target culture will be a balancing act between the need to find appropriate sounds and connotations, the need to mark the nationality of the product, and also the need to avoid unnecessary costs in packaging and advertising, although retaining the source language name may be seen as cultural imperialism.

Thus, borrowing may sound superficially unproblematic: if the target language doesn't have a word for something, just borrow it from a language that does. But it is not as simple as that; it raises important questions of national identity, power and colonization. Since the collapse of the Soviet Union, the Russian language has, to the dismay of some, borrowed American words almost greedily; German has long been replete with English loan terms even where German terms already exist; and the French authorities make regular attempts to de-americanize their language.

Calque

A calque is a literal translation at the level of the phrase (Vinay and Darbelnet do not consider its use at the morphemic level in translating terminology). The most frequently cited examples are the various translations of *skyscraper*. According to Fedorov, calques tend to come into the language together with the thing they refer to (we will question this in a moment). He quotes the example of *gromkovoritel*, a literal Russian translation of *loudspeaker* (1953:163). When the Russians first had to deal with supermarkets they did so through the calque *svierkhrynok*, but this proved to be ambiguous and so was replaced by 'shop without assistants' before becoming 'self-service shop' (Retsker 1974:12).

Like borrowings, calques often make their first appearance not in translations but as an element in a newspaper article or in some other form of original literature, since journalists and creative writers tend more often than translators to see themselves as word creators. Although no research has been done to prove this, it seems highly likely that translators will resort more readily to borrowing than to calque, since the guidelines for using the latter are far less obvious than for the former.

Despite Fedorov's claim, calques do not always appear at the same time as the thing. The oil crisis that did so much economic damage in the 1970s used to be referred to in the English press as just that. In the

1990s the posher press began to talk about the *oil shock*. For decades the English language used the phrase *both sides of industry*, but Eurospeak has since introduced *the social partners*, and now economic commentators use *Anglo-Saxon* to mean *English and American*, These are all late calques from the French, proving that interlingual influence is a two-way street after all.

Literal translation

This is the rare but always welcome case when a text can go from one language into another with no changes other than those required by the target-language grammar. Vinay and Darbelnet do not say much about this, so we have to turn to Vázquez-Ayora for such things as the distinction between literal translation as a legitimate translation technique and literal translation as a general strategy, which he castigates as mechanistic and servile. He describes the technique as follows:

> If, given two utterances, one in English and the other in Spanish, there exists between them a precise correspondence of 'structure' and of 'signification', and the equivalence is achieved moneme by moneme, literal translation results and can be applied without risk.

And he adds the dire warning: "The translator should not alter this process out of an itch to change things or out of simple fear of the criticism (from the ignorant) that the translation is literal in the pejorative sense of the term" (1977:257). He gives a number of examples that require only obligatory grammatical adjustments, concluding that they are legitimate cases of literal translation, which he calls the "degree zero of translation" (1977:258). He compares, for example, *John hit Paul / Juan pegó a Pablo*, which are literal translations (the *a* is an obligatory addition in Spanish), with *I have a headache / Me duele la cabeza*, where the lexemes 'me', 'hurt', 'head' are translated but in a radically different grammatical structure (1977:258). This is called 'oblique' translation, and more specifically transposition, and is used alongside the remaining translation techniques when a literal translation:

i   gives another meaning;
ii   has no meaning;
iii is structurally impossible;
iv   corresponds to nothing in the target-language metalinguistics;
v   does have a target-language correspondence but not at the
     same language level. (Vinay and Darbelnet 1958:49)

Transposition

The technique of transposition is how Vinay and Darbelnet deal with grammatical changes in translation. Both they and Vázquez-Ayora devote some considerable space to the not always fascinating task of demonstrating how the parts of speech may play musical chairs in translation. Unexciting though such lists may be, they contain information that can be of use to novice translators. Some students might, for example, translate the French *l'économie n'a cessé de croître* by the very clumsy *the economy did not stop growing* when, in fact, it needs a verb/adverb transposition (*the economy grew steadily*) or a point-of-view reversal (*the economy continued to grow*).

Of course such a shift does not constitute a rule – one of the main criticisms made against Vinay and Darbelnet is that they give precisely that false impression. For example, they propose *in the early 19th century* as a translation of *au début du 19e siècle*, but the context may require one to translate it more literally. Support for their proposed translation comes twice in the opening scene of Buñuel's film *Milky Way*, where *à la fin du Nième siècle* is subtitled as *in the late Nth century*, but this may simply have been an economy imposed by the medium.

Some of the information contained in the kind of list provided by Vinay and Darbelnet or Vázquez-Ayora is purely grammatical, more a matter of language knowledge than translation competence. In the same list as the 'n'a cessé de' example, Vinay and Darbelnet also include the French verb *faillir* in its meaning of the English adverbial 'almost/nearly'; but this is the only meaning it can have, which makes it a matter of langue, whereas the decision to translate *cesser* as a verb or an adverb will depend on a number of factors, making it an act of parole.

Modulation

This is defined by Vinay and Darbelnet as "a variation in the message, obtained by changing point of view, lighting" (1958:51). As Vázquez-Ayora (1977:293) says, many translators use transposition intuitively but the use of modulation, which requires extensive knowledge of the target language, is far less obvious and more risky. The idea, as explained by Kelly (1979:133), is that the signifier changes while the signified remains the same, and this is achieved by various forms of metaphor, metonymy and synecdoche. Modulation may take place between such things as an abstract and a concrete term, between a part and a whole, or it may reverse a point of view. Vinay and Darbelnet (1958:236-8) quote such examples as *give a pint of blood / donnez un peu de votre sang* (concrete-to-abstract), *you're quite a stranger*

/ *on ne se voit plus* (effect-to-cause), *from cover to cover* / *de la première à la dernière page* (part-to-part), *you can have it* / *je vous le laisse* (reversal of terms), to which we can add *vous avez bien cinq minutes* / *you can spare a moment* (rethinking of time intervals), while Vázquez-Ayora gives us *would give him some ideas* / *le ayudarían a pensar* (result-to-means), *don't get so excited* / *tranquilízate* (negated opposite, two other examples of which occur in the subtitles of Buñuel's *Milky Way*: *il ne fait pas chaud ce soir* / *it's a bit chilly tonight* and *ce n'est pas trop tôt* / *about time*), which are also antonymic translations, of course.

Équivalence

Vinay and Darbelnet define *équivalence* essentially as the translation of idioms when two languages refer to the same situation in totally different ways. As such, it is not, in their presentation, an especially interesting translation case since it is based essentially on language knowledge. You either know or do not know how to translate phrases like *as thick as two short planks* or *to have jelly belly*. If you do not (and if your dictionary doesn't come to your rescue) then no amount of theory will help. When a translator does fail to spot an idiom and translates its elements separately, we have what Vinay and Darbelnet call 'overtranslation' (1958:31).

The interesting problem with *équivalence* arises, as Fedorov (1953:171) points out, in cases such as literature and advertising when the idiom is motivated (is based on a structural or situational feature) but has no correspondence in the target language. An example of this occurred in *The Observer* newspaper of 15 December 1996 which gave a literal translation of the French expression 'He who steals an *œuf* [egg] will also steal a *bœuf* [ox]'.

In such cases choices have to be made between translating the basic meaning or attempting to convey some of the flavour of the original. Fedorov (1953:172) quotes the example of a Romany idiom meaning 'flies can't get into a closed mouth' based on assonance between *panda* (mouth) and *macha* (flies). This would be difficult to achieve in English, but in French a literal translation actually strengthens the effect by turning assonance to rhyme (*bouche* / *mouche*). The Russian translation has to alter the meaning slightly to achieve the same effect: 'into a mouth closed tight (*glukho*) fly no flies (*mukha*)'. In another case quoted by Fedorov (1953:173), the translator modified the original to achieve a phrase that is not actually a Russian idiom but a very convincing imitation of one: the French 'empty barrels sing best' becomes 'an empty barrel rings more resoundingly', which, according to Fedorov, "evokes the impression of a living phrasal combination that could have existed in Russian".

One problem with the concept of *équivalence* is the term itself, which now has a much wider meaning in translation. This is why some people prefer to keep the word in its French form.

Adaptation

Adaptation is the final translation technique on Vinay and Darbelnet's list, and the one most open to controversy. This is demonstrated quite ironically by the two authors themselves. Having outlined the techniques, they provide examples in tabular form of each one applied at each linguistic level (1958:55):

i at the lexical level they propose translating *cyclisme* by either *baseball* or *cricket*, even though they themselves refer to the confusion caused when an interpreter translated *cricket* as *Tour de France*;

ii at the syntactic level they offer *before you could say Jack Robinson* for *en un clin d'œil*, presumably called adaptation rather than équivalence because of the Englishness of 'Jack Robinson', even though it is precisely this which makes such a translation problematic in some contexts;

iii at the message level they actually seem to propose translating the French *bon appétit* (enjoy your meal) by the American *Hi!*, which needs no further comment.

This kind of substitution is supposed to take place when the receiving culture has little or nothing in its experience that would allow it to understand a close translation. Vázquez-Ayora (1977:324) quotes Nida's example of the absurdity of translating *white as snow* for a culture which has no knowledge of the substance, a problem referred to in the musical *The King and I*. Adapting this to a comparison with white bird plumage may seem quite a reasonable solution. However, Vázquez-Ayora also shows how problematic adaptation can be when he refers approvingly to a suggestion by Vinay and Darbelnet (1958:53) that it is culturally normal for English fathers, but not for French fathers, to kiss their daughters on the mouth (albeit only when returning home after a long journey!). There is no indication where this idea comes from but it is highly doubtful if such behaviour was ever the case, and it would certainly raise eyebrows nowadays. This demonstrates the extreme delicacy of resorting to adaptation and the extensive knowledge one needs of other cultures before even thinking of using it.

Similar confusion is likely to arise from a case of adaptation in the translation of the film *Une Semaine de vacances*, where the subtitler has replaced a reference to a Belgian joke by a reference to an Irish joke, since it was customary, in pre-political correctness days, to use these nationalities in France and England respectively as examples of low intelligence. There are two dangers here which typify all adaptation. Firstly, people with no knowledge of the source culture get the wrong idea about it and come away with the belief that French people tell jokes about the Irish, which may serve to reinforce prejudice. Secondly, they learn nothing about the cultures of other people. In the extreme case, adaptation leads to what Levý calls 'localization and topicalization' (1969:86), which can be a high-risk strategy if it has not been specifically commissioned.

Vinay and Darbelnet suggest that such items should be adapted to the receiving culture unless the translator is looking for what they disparagingly call "cheap local colour" (1958:53) in the style of 'The muzhik finished his kasha and kefir and jumped into his kibitka'. Their preferred strategy of adaptation is a dangerous one, but there are times when it may be appropriate. A text on the quality of life published in *Le Monde* many years ago symbolized degrees of decorum by referring to different methods of payment in French restaurants: in cheap eateries the bill is scribbled on the plain paper tablecloth; in establishments seeking a higher social tone the tablecloth will be embossed paper; while in the very best restaurants the bill will be brought on a saucer. In cultures where such a practice does not exist, it might be thought more important to adapt this text to local habits, since the purpose of the text is to make a moral point rather than communicate knowledge about French lifestyles. In the same text, however, it might be thought tasteless to try to adapt a reference to the French town of Oradour, the site of Nazi atrocities during the Second World War. In such cases there are techniques other than adaptation available to the translator.

The fact that Vinay and Darbelnet, as well as other linguistically-oriented translation theorists, do consider matters of culture shows that Lefevere is quite wrong when he claims that "linguists have moved from word to text as a unit, but not beyond" (Bassnett and Lefevere 1990:4). They may not have taken the 'cultural turn' in his own meaning of ideological manipulation in translation, but they do not ignore the world beyond the word.

Although the work of Vinay and Darbelnet has been criticized from many sides, as we shall see below, it is true to say that theirs was a pioneering work and Delisle is right to say that it had "resounding and well-deserved success" (1988:75), at least in the French and Canadian tradition. They are also referred to in the Russian and Spanish literature (the latter largely because of the work of Vázquez-Ayora). Yet this is not quite so true of the Anglo-American domain. Two of the most widely read English books on translation theory are Newmark's *Approaches to Translation*, where Vinay and Darbelnet are mentioned just twice, and Nida and Taber's *The Theory and Practice of Translation*, where their name appears only in the bibliography. It remains to be seen whether that situation will be remedied by the appearance, almost forty years on, of an English translation of their work.

An American model

In addition to the seven translation techniques listed above, Vinay and Darbelnet refer to the concepts of 'dilution'/'concentration' and 'amplification'/'economy' (1958:183-188). These notions also surface in a translation taxonomy devised thirty years later by Malone, who describes the further techniques (or 'trajections' as he calls them) of 'matching', 'zigzagging', 'recrescence', 'repackaging', 'reordering' and 'recoding'. His claim (1988:2) is that such techniques and procedures will "serve either as tools for the study of completed translation (the ANALYTIC mode), or as helpmates in the act of translation (the OPERATIVE mode)."

Most of these translation processes are described by three terms: the generic term listed above and two specific terms. Thus, the generic process Matching (Malone capitalizes the words) covers two specific processes called Equation and Substitution. However, the two specific processes do not exhaust all the possibilities of the generic process so the latter are also discussed in their own right.

Matching: Substitution and Equation

Equation is the same as Vinay and Darbelnet's 'literal translation' and so needs no further discussion here. Where it is not possible, it is replaced by Substitution which encompasses Vinay and Darbelnet's transposition (for example, a Greek grammatical structure signalling prayer Substituted by the archaic pronoun *thou*), équivalence (the German idiom 'the air was clear' Substituted by *the way was clear*), and adaptation (having a character in a poem hum rather than whistle because the latter is not seen as 'poetic') (1988:20-21).

The generic process for Equation and Substitution is Matching (1988:22), which takes two forms:

i   alternation between Equation and Substitution for stylistic reasons;
ii   replacement by something that is neither Equation nor Substitution.

An example of (i) is where a translator introduces stylistic variation into what is called a co-reference chain. A child might write a story in the

form *John got up early. John was going fishing. John liked fishing* where
an adult might write *John got up early. He was going fishing. The lad was
a keen fan of the sport*, varying the modes of reference to *John* and *fishing*
through the chain of sentences to avoid tedium. As Baker (1992:183) says,
"Each language has what we might call general preferences for certain patterns of reference as well as specific preferences that are sensitive to text
type". Very little is known about this, so most translators will act intuitively.
If a varied co-reference chain is not or cannot be maintained in translation,
then equivalence at text level is not achieved.

Examples of (ii), where the Matching consists neither of Equation nor
Substitution, begin with our old friends 'borrowing' (which Malone calls
'carry-over matching') and 'calque', plus 'prefabricated matching' and 'faux
amis' (1988:23).

In our earlier discussion we mentioned borrowing only as a one-way
street from source to target language, as when German television dubbers
provide local colour by borrowing *Sir* and *Mister* in the translation of American TV series. But a source-language text can itself contain borrowings.
Again, in original German TV series one can hear things like *Das war too
much* ('It was too much') and *das ist die ganze Cleverness* ('that's the
whole cleverness'). When texts containing such items are translated into
English, the foreignizing effect is simply lost.

Malone's concept of prefabricated matching refers to the use of already
existing, conventionalized target-language counterparts (1988:26), as when
the Latin *auri* is translated by *burnisht gold* rather than just *gold* because of
the prevailing poetics. This is the kind of thing Toury (1995:267-68) is
referring to with his 'law of growing standardisation' according to which
source language textemes are replaced by target language repertoremes or
linguistic routines. It is this process which gives unity of expression to the
translations of a given era.

Such pre-fabricated conventions may actually be the result of translation activity, giving what Steiner (1992:333) calls "the 'moon in pond like
blossom weary' school of instant exotica". Alternatively, the conventions
may derive from overt or covert authoritarian imposition, as with the translation of Freud. Hatim and Mason (1990b:2) tell us that the English
translators tried to make Freud conform to the norms of scientific discourse,
using Latin to translate his very Germanic lexis for example, while Hjort
writes that "a translator ... who is informed about the history of Freud
translation knows that he or she will be expected to follow certain conventions" (in Bassnett and Lefevere 1990:43). In the mid-1990s the French
written media reported the furore surrounding the latest Freud translation
for the same reasons.

The category of 'faux amis' is somewhat out of place in Malone's list of trajections (1988:28), since they really constitute translation errors. They are source-language words that look like target-language words but which mean different things. They are a fact of the language system not of translation competence. A translator who is taken in by them simply has more language learning to do. Hönig and Kussmaul (1984:120) ask "Why are there so many curates and so few vicars in England? Why do Americans build houses so huge that visitors go in and find themselves standing in a lobby?" The answer is that novice German translators are tricked by the spelling into thinking that *hall* means *Halle* (German for 'hotel lobby') and *vicar* means *Vikar* (German for 'curate').

Zigzagging: Divergence and Convergence

This set of trajections arises from different lexical structuring between languages that we discussed earlier, leading to the concept of one-to-many equivalence. The German word *See* Diverges into English *sea* or *lake*, while the German *Wurst* Diverges into *sausage* or *turd*. This again is a matter of language knowledge and important only to novice translators who have to learn to read the linguistic, situational and stylistic clues that will tell them the correct meaning.

However, such disambiguation into Divergence is not always easy, often because dictionaries are out-of-date or incomplete (a fact which too many student translators bizarrely refuse to accept). Many French-English dictionaries give only one meaning for the word *populisme* (a literary movement), completely omitting its political meaning, and so inducing error in students who believe the dictionary never lies.

More interesting from the point of view of translation are those situations where Divergence is a source-language stylistic choice that cannot always be replicated in the target language. In certain English newspapers, quotations are often followed by some colourful phrase expressing the speaker's attitude, such as *he stormed* or *he complained*, whereas in other languages the range may be rather more restricted ('he declared', 'he said'). Such cases require the translator to have considerable textual competence in the target language, including knowledge of the type of publication involved. By comparing the British *Financial Times* with the French *Le Figaro*, Gallagher (1993:153) concludes that it is the British newspaper which has a more restricted set of choices in this situation. He might have found different results with different publications.

Divergence may have unwanted side effects. An author may use a device such as ambiguity to create suspense which the target language may not be able to replicate because it must Diverge into unambiguous terms. Malone (1988:34) quotes a use of the pronoun *us* which produces deliberate uncertainty because we do not know who is included in it. This effect is lost in languages that have no such ambiguous terms for the word.

The French text on the quality of life referred to earlier starts with the French word for 'it' and then uses a variety of other devices such as 'of which' and 'of it' to avoid saying what the text is about until the very last word of a long paragraph. It is open to debate whether such a device can be sustained in English or must be destroyed by early Divergence. As de Beaugrande and Dressler say, this linguistic occurrence works best "if the distance between the pro-form and the co-referring expression is kept within limits" (1981:61), and the impetuous English might find a whole paragraph too much to stomach.

A text beginning with *Il s'agit juste d'un petit test réalisé par Fortune* uses the impersonal text opener 'it is a matter of' to delay the topic of a test carried out by *Fortune*, creating a small moment of suspense and a note of irony (the test measures the risk of being made redundant). If the target language cannot replicate this structure, either by turning the sentence round (*Fortune magazine has devised this little test*) or by using a different presentational device (*There's this little test* ...), the effect may have to be lost with *il* and *test* Diverging into something like 'questionnaire/test'.

Malone (1988:88) also quotes the possibility of Divergence into one or another target term (paradigmatic Divergence) being replaced by syntagmatic Divergence in which the translator strings together all possible translations. In our discussion of compensation we referred to the untranslatable pun in *le socialisme français est un cadavre exquis*. Rather than forcing ourselves to choose just one of its possible meanings, we could put both: *The mish-mash that is French socialism is well and truly dead.* This technique could clearly become all too safe a haven for the indecisive.

The opposite of Divergence is Convergence, where varied source-language terms collapse into just one in the target language, in many cases a simple fact of life calling for no special action from the translator except if the original diversity served a purpose such as the expression of status: Wienold (1990:184) quotes the case of the translation of a Japanese dialogue between a young woman and an old man Converging to give the impression of equal status where the original showed deference.

Zigzagging is the generic term for Divergence and Convergence. These are situations where the source language has what are called doublets, two words meaning the same thing but often with some kind of connotational difference. According to Malone (1988:38) Norwegian has two words for a smoker's pipe, a standard word and a word more expressive of personal attachment. Vinay and Darbelnet (1958:72-73) show zigzagging between the French *maternel* and the English *maternal / motherly*, and also claim that the two languages systematically operate a technical/normal register switch as in *concours hippique / horse show*.

Perhaps the best application of Zigzagging would be to describe situations where the translator has a choice between Divergence and Convergence. Many languages economically convey information about gender. A sentence such as the French *je suis fatiguée* tells us the speaker is a woman. In translation this would usually Converge into the genderless *I'm tired*. But if the translator feels the reader should know the speaker's gender (this was the first sentence in the text), some form of Divergence/Diffusion would have to be found: *I'm one very tired lady/woman* are possible, but they alter the meaning in a number of ways.

Recrescence: Amplification and Reduction

This rather surgically named set of techniques is more or less self-explanatory. Amplification is what we should use instead of Vinay and Darbelnet's politically suspicious 'adaptation' technique, providing explanations rather than making cultural adaptations as a strategy for bridging anticipated gaps in the target-language audience's knowledge. The extent to which it happens will depend on the translator's attitude to the readership and to hard work.

Some translators believe in giving readers no assistance whatsoever, insisting that they should use dictionaries and encyclopaedias, while other translators are overly lavish with disruptive footnotes. Govaert (1971:431) warns that explicitation must be justified by the micro- and macro-context, "otherwise the translator is embellishing and tampering". We shall see an example of what he means below.

In relation to the question of hard work, translators will show varying degrees of willingness to undertake research to supplement their own knowledge gaps. Trainee translators in particular seem quite happy to use only the means immediately to hand, rather than going off to research more widely. What is one to think of the translator who was content to produce the sentence *It reminded many people of the story of the Medusa raft*, which would in fact remind most readers of nothing at all? Similarly, the translator who produced *according to 'Monarchs and Cannibals' by Marvin Harris* from a French original was foolish to assume that the book title required no more than literal translation (the non-Gallic name should have rung warning bells), when in fact the original title was *Of Cannibals and Kings*.

Malone lists a number of text types that might require the use of Amplification, although ultimately of course all text types may require it. His list includes philosophical texts, for which Zimmer (1981:118-20) provides an example taken from the translation by the German philosopher Schleiermacher of a Platonic dialogue on a subject we mentioned in Chapter 1 about the link between signifier and signified being arbitrary or motivated. Is there something about a word that makes it uniquely appropriate for the object it designates? One of the speakers in the Platonic text says yes, arguing that the Greek word *anthropos* ('man') is the perfect term to use because it is made up of two words meaning 'examine' and 'observe' (*anathrei* and *opope* in Greek), which is what distinguishes humans from animals, making the word just perfect. Now, Schleiermacher happened to have his own theory of translation in which literal translation is given pride of place, and he translated the passage according to his principles. However, the result makes no sense because the German words for 'man', 'look' and 'observe' are no more related than their English equivalents. The text needed some form of Amplification.

Providing the target audience with enough information to understand the translation can be a headache because the translator has to make often difficult judgements about the readers' level of sophistication and the degree to which they can be expected to show initiative, while trying to balance out such things as information overload and readability. Again these are matters that take translational decision-making beyond the linguistic dimension into such matters as cultural judgements and publishing policy.

Many of the cases where a translator may consider using Amplification concern world knowledge, and since they compensate for knowledge gaps Malone calls them 'compensatory Amplifications'.

Amplifications of this type can range from the addition of just one or two words in the body of the text (*the French trade union CGT, the German newspaper Die Zeit*), to footnotes and even appendices. How much information would be required, for example, to Amplify the reference to the Medusa raft quoted above? Not as much as the two whole volumes of footnotes supplied by the author Vladimir Nabokov to explain his literal translation of the nineteenth-century epic poem *Eugene Onegin*.

There are, however, cases of Amplification motivated by linguistic reasons. Malone (1988:45) calls these 'classificatory Amplifications' because they indicate that the word is one of a set. The word *old* may be added in front of a nickname as a way of putting the word in its class, as also happened in the student translation *it was the modern version of the old shipwreck story* where there was no equivalent for *old* in the source language. Under this heading one might also reclassify the device referred to earlier of amplifying an awkward source-language plural noun into a phrase by adding words like *kinds, types, methods* etc. In a French text about food safety we are told about the hysterical behaviour of *certaines volailles*, where the best translation strategy would be to write *some breeds of poultry*.

Reduction is the omission of information considered to be unnecessary, of little importance, or unlikely to make sense to the target-language reader. The text *les top-models, comme disent les Anglais* does not need the last four words translated into English, just as the text *the cadres – the white-collar, middle-class workers – are dissatisfied* can do without the explanation in a translation into French. Malone (1988:47) quotes the example of *Plakate an Litfaßsäulen* ('bills or posters on columns or pillars') translated simply as *bills* because columns specifically for displaying advertisements are less usual in Britain and the United States, whereas the French have a ready-made equivalent in *colonne Morris*. Another solution to the problem can be to use Diffusion into a definition, which can then be reduced back into shorter form in later recurrences. This is often the preferred solution for dealing with an institution commonly referred to by an acronym: the steps are to Diffuse the acronym into its full form, Amplify by explaining the function of the institution, and then Reduce future references back down to the acronym: *The SDKPiL (The Social-Democratic Party of Poland and Lithuania) was set up in ... Members of the SDKPiL ...* Sometimes step one is omitted, as in *DGSE (the French equivalent of MI6)*.

Recrescence is the generic term for Amplification and Reduction. Like Zigzagging, it seems not to refer to a different phenomenon but rather to cases where Amplification and Reduction alternate under the pressure of different demands.

Repackaging: Diffusion and Condensation

Whereas Amplification and Reduction add or remove information, Diffusion and Condensation express the same information in longer or shorter form.

These four terms are mirrored in Vinay and Darbelnet's 'amplification/ economy' and 'dilution/concentration' (1958:183-88). The difference is that Vinay and Darbelnet see amplification/economy not so much as providing/ omitting useful/pointless information for the target-language reader but as characteristics of specific languages: English is more concise than French, they say, when it is describing 'reality', while French is more 'rapid' when writing about the intellect (1958:188). A second difference is that their examples do not always allow one to see the distinction. It is not entirely clear, for example, why *bilan* represents a 'concentration' in relation to the diluted *balance sheet*, while *haut* represents an 'economy' in relation to the amplified *this side up* (1958:183,185).

Diffusion can occur for two reasons, one structural and related to linguistic competence, the other properly translational. A book like *Languages of Asia and the Pacific* is replete with examples of lexical diffusion: the one word *fail* becomes the two-word *tidak dapat* in Malay; *complain* becomes *bulpyong ul mal hamnida* in Korean; Spanish can say in one word (*matear*) what it takes five words to say in English (*to plant at regular intervals*).

Such structural Diffusion can arise for grammatical reasons also. One use of the French conditional and the German subjunctive is to signal that the writer is reporting someone else's words without supporting or denying them. In many other languages, this would have to be Diffused into *According to ...* or *It is claimed that ...*, a fact not realized by two journalists from *The Guardian* newspaper who translated it as a standard conditional (Hatim and Mason 1990a:83). Clearly, this kind of Diffusion and Concentration will be frequent and banal translation procedures because of the nature of language.

Diffusion becomes a matter for proper translation decision-making in cases where a complex concept is lexicalized in one language but not in another, as with the German *Familienanschluß*. The dictionary Diffuses this into the definition or description *where one is treated as one of the family*, but other Diffusions are possible and may be preferable (*a friendly, caring firm* comes to mind). Such definitional Diffusion is often appropriate in conjunction with borrowing when the context offers no clues to help the target-language reader divine what the borrowing means.

One kind of Diffusion for which there is no reason or excuse is quoted by Govaert (1971:431-32). He compares an extract from a Dutch novel with its French translation. The original Dutch says:

> He was only the guide of this famous traveller, who had published thick books, and wrote incredibly rapidly in his notebook in a sort of shorthand that nobody could understand.

And the French translation says:

> He was in fact only a guide and nothing more, a guide being paid by this tourist, who was thought in the valley to be a writer of renown; some even claimed that he had already published some very, very fat books. And why not? Could he not be seen at every moment opening his notebook to scribble notes in it and cover the paper, with incredible speed, with complicated signs that were absolutely incomprehensible.

Condensation is less frequent than Diffusion according to Malone, which may seem surprising since it should simply depend on the direction of translation. What he seems to mean by this claim is the 'fact' that translations are nearly always longer than the originals because of the need precisely for Amplification and Diffusion. I put 'fact' in inverted commas because it is not clear if this often repeated commonplace about translation has ever been subjected to proper testing. Vinay and Darbelnet (1958:185) are just two of many authors who make the claim, attributing it to prudence and ignorance, but they offer no proof.

One use of Condensation over the ages concerns the sometimes perceived need to cut out parts of the text that might be thought boring, obscene or politically problematic. Although a study of Condensation from this point of view is extremely interesting, and we shall refer to it again, it is obviously not a matter for linguistics.

Repackaging, the generic term for Diffusion and Concentration, again refers to the process of shifting between the two in the course of translating a text be in response to a variety of pressures such as the need to build in more detail early in a text and then find shorter ways of referring to the same thing to avoid prolixity, the need to extricate oneself from complicated sentence structures, the need to accommodate rhetorical structures, the need to vary co-reference chains, and so on.

Reordering

Malone's final 'trajection' is Reordering. His rather short discussion simply enumerates and exemplifies situations where reordering word sequences becomes necessary for comprehension, as in the breaking up of complex structures, or because the source and target languages have different narrative and stylistic structures.

The subject is also covered somewhat more extensively by Vinay and Darbelnet under two headings:

i   *Word order*, which tends to be fixed by the grammar of the language, so that we cannot nowadays, in English, say *Where go you?*, whereas we could say *What say you?*, but it would not mean the same thing, being either ironic anachronism or meaning *What do you think?*

ii   What Vinay and Darbelnet call *la démarche*, a word that is not easy to translate except by a diffusional 'order of doing things', which presents more freedom of choice than word order and has to do with the specific 'spirit' of a language. Since French is what they call a *langue de l'entendement*, in other words one that represents the order of reality in a logical order in the sentence, it proceeds by announcing the subject and then saying something about it. They say this tendency is so strong in French that it has the side effect that adverbial phrases of time, manner and place gravitate towards the beginning, since they merely modulate the message without being the main point. English, being what they call a 'language of the concrete', more 'touchy-feely' as it were, does not have the same compulsion to announce causes before effects. Consequently, where the French would (and English could) say 'Being ready, he set off on his travels', English is more likely to say 'He set off on his travels when he was ready'.

Although this kind of statement needs considerable hedging because all sorts of combinations may be possible in phrasal placing in sentences, it is given some support by the ludicrously melodramatic translation 'But who, in Auckland harbour on the evening of July 10, placed two mines on the hull of the *Rainbow Warrior?*' (quoted in Hatim and Mason 1990a:87), where what is a normal order of presentation in French sounds in English like a botched attempt at creating suspense.

Critique

A number of criticisms have been levelled at such taxonomies, especially that of Vinay and Darbelnet, which is the oldest. They can be grouped under five headings:

1. The nature of the categories: authorities such as Chuquet and Paillard (1987:10), Kelly (1979:133) and Larose (1989:18) point out that some of the categories (borrowing, calque) are not really translation techniques at all, while others (adaptation) go way beyond translation, and the remainder are not clearly distinguishable from one another. However, if we are to make some sort of systemic sense out of translation (which is the aim of a linguistic approach), you have to start somewhere, and it is surely significant that different researchers come up with broadly comparable categories.
2. The taxonomies have more to do with contrastive linguistics than with the dynamics of translation, and as such they register facts of more importance to language learners than to translators. The discussion above should have shown that this is only partly true.
3. Even though the taxonomists describe their categories as translation 'techniques' or 'processes', they are actually nothing of the sort (Delisle 1988:72-73). They are after-the-event categories for describing the end result of the translation process and not, as Malone claims, operational procedures guiding the process itself. There are two answers to this.

Firstly, even if that is all they were, they would still be important. Describing translations systematically has been invaluable to modern translation theory (and trainee translators should have to practise it). Kitty van Leuven-Zwart (1989, 1990) has welded her own version of Vinay and Darbelnet's taxonomy to the concept of 'shift' developed in a literary approach to translation with a view to establishing the existence of translation norms, while the present author (1997) has used it to trace the workings of a colonialist mindset in translation.

Secondly, whether these taxonomies describe product or process is a matter of viewpoint. Once you have learnt, for example, that it is possible to do an antonymic translation and seen how it works, then it does become a translation process to be used with all the other skills a translator deploys.

4. The taxonomies are not predictive. Knowing what the translation techniques are does not tell you when to use them. This criticism would be important if one wanted to claim that translation is a science, a piece of hubris that few would now be guilty of.

5. The taxonomies are just fancy names for what translators already do (or think they do) intuitively; learning them would therefore be a waste of time. This is a serious objection. Kelly (1979:155) concludes from his analysis of translation over the centuries that translators were indeed applying these techniques before the linguists named them, while Malone (1988:150) admits the absurdity of supposing that a particular translation was arrived at by the conscious use of one of his techniques.

In the meantime, however, a lot of translation still has a bad press, as exemplified by the currency of the pejorative word *translationese* and the frequency with which translations are dissected and found wanting at academic conferences and in the press. *The Observer* of 8 January 1995 talked of "drab duds" and "one enormous disaster" in reference to translation, and just over a year later referred to "a cumbersome translation from the French", adding "If there is such a thing as kitsch translation, this is it".

The problem is often seen to be inappropriate literalism. One reason for this may be that translators who have never have learnt to think of such things as 'hypernymic' or 'antonymic' translation in any systematic way have an impoverished vocabulary to talk to themselves about what they are doing. We shall see in the section on psycholinguistics that translators may monologue with themselves when they are translating, especially in difficult spots. Maybe the quality of their translations could be improved by enriching the quality of their monologues, to the extent that they can replace vague concepts such as 'sounds right', 'clumsy' and 'flow' by a more precise vocabulary.

Komissarov (1977:46) is no doubt right when he says the ability to translate does not mean the ability to formulate one's thought processes explicitly in this way. But he also says that a translator's intuitive ideas on translation may be false. Rejecting translation theory on the grounds that 'it's just putting fancy names to what I do already' is perfectly acceptable if translators are indeed 'doing these things already' and doing them well. But if not, then knowing the names and practising the techniques of translation, having a 'science' of translation to start with, may correct the deficiencies and the wrong intuitions, creating à liberating effect without being a constraint. The 'art' of translation comes from the accumulated experience of enriching and applying the 'science' of translation.

5. Equivalence

The ultimate goal of the various translation techniques and strategies outlined in the previous chapter is to achieve 'equivalence', a concept that has probably cost the lives of more trees than any other in translation studies. Why this is so becomes obvious when you consider the five 'frames of reference' listed by Koller (1979:188-89) as constituting word and text meaning and which, in an ideal world, would have to be accounted for in order to say that particular kinds of equivalence have been achieved:

1. denotational meaning: the object or concept referred to (hence also called referential meaning);

2. connotational meaning, which Koller breaks down into nine sub-categories:

> language level (elevated, poetic, formal, normal, familiar, colloquial, slang, vulgar)
> sociolect (the 'jargon' of different social groups such as soldiers, students, etc.)
> dialect (the language of a particular region)
> medium (written versus spoken language)
> style (old-fashioned, trendy, euphemistic, etc.)
> frequency (common versus rare words)
> domain (normal, scientific, technical)
> value (positive versus negative)
> emotional tone (neutral, cold, warm, etc.)

3. textual norms (the kind of language typical of such things as legal texts or instructions for use, etc.)

4. pragmatic meaning (reader expectations)

5. linguistic form (rhyme, rhythm, metaphor, etc.).

Matching a shopping list of this kind, and perhaps even more importantly, getting two different translators to match it and to come up with exactly the same solution (the wrong desideratum but one apparently espoused by many critics of the concept of equivalence) is clearly such an impossible task that the concept seems dubious, especially when presented as a quasi-mathematical notion, as it sometimes has been. Snell-Hornby (1988:22) takes the view that "equivalence is unsuitable as a basic concept in translation theory" because it is "imprecise and ill-defined (even after a heated debate of over twenty years)".

The stakes in relation to the concept of equivalence are high. When Kelly (1979:24) asks "What does the linguist have to offer the translator?", his answer is "The most obvious is analysis of equivalence, and some objective justification of the translator's intuitions".

There have been many definitions of equivalence, and it would be tedious to go through them all here. The most famous are probably those of Catford and Nida.

Catford and textual equivalence

Catford deserves a mention, even though Snell-Hornby (1988:14-15) believes his approach "is now generally considered dated and of mere historical interest". He describes equivalence as a 'key term' and tells us that "The central problem of translation practice is that of finding TL |target-language] translation equivalents. A central problem of translation theory is that of defining the nature and conditions of translation equivalence" (1965:21).

Catford makes a distinction between formal correspondence and what he calls 'textual equivalence' (1965:27), but this is not necessarily a distinction between two approaches to translation. Formal correspondence is a matter of langue whereas textual equivalence is a matter of parole. Formal correspondence exists where a target-language category occupies the same position in its language system as the same or some other category in the source language. Thus prepositions seem to operate in the same way in most European languages (1965:32-33). In so far as we can translate preposition by preposition in these languages, formal correspondence gives us textual equivalence. Where that is not the case, we arrive at textual equivalence through translation 'shifts' (1965:73).

These can be structure shifts (*John loves Mary* becomes 'Is love at John on Mary' in Gaelic), class shifts (the adjective in *medical student* becomes an adverbial phrase in the French equivalent 'student in medicine'), unit shifts (the English indefinite article translated by a change in word order in Russian), and intra-system shifts (a source-language singular becomes a target-language plural). This is Catford's own taxonomy of translation techniques, comparable to those seen earlier, but much more restricted because the terms are based rigorously on a purely linguistic system.

On one point Catford is adamant. In translation, either through formal correspondence or through textual equivalence achieved by translation shifts, we do not transfer meaning between languages. What we do is *replace* a source-language meaning by a target-language meaning that can function in the same way in the situation being represented linguistically. He demonstrates that two equivalent utterances in a source language and a target language do *not* have the same meaning because languages will verbalize different situational features: showing the speaker is a woman, signalling modes of transport, expressing respect, indicating verbal aspect, and so on. Catford goes on to state that textual equivalence is achieved when the source and target items are *"interchangeable in a given situation"* (1965:49, Catford's italics) and this happens when *'an SL [source-language] and a TL [target-language] text or item are relatable to (at least some of) the same features of substance'* (1965:50, Catford's italics).

The reference to substance may seem a little odd, but it stems from the linguistic theory Catford is working with. Writing, sound and the things out there in the world are 'substance'. Language is an abstract and formal representation of that substance. Taking his rather simple example, the Russian *ya prishla* (I came/have come) uses a formal means (the final *-a* on *prishla*) to represent the situational substance that the speaker is a woman. There is nothing about the substance of a woman that requires her to be represented by the sound/letter *-a*. That is a matter of abstract linguistic form, as is also the fact that, in a situation where we are describing somebody arriving in a place, Russian will use formal means to pick out from the situational substance the notion of gender and the mode of transport, French may formally signal gender (*je suis arrivée*) but not transport mode, German will signal transport mode (*kommen* vs. *fahren*) but not gender, while English will signal neither, but all three can be textual equivalents in the appropriate situation.

The way different languages choose which elements of the situation to represent and which to ignore is part of the differential slicing up of reality which we talked about in Chapter 3. Although, according to Catford's theory, textual equivalence is the solution, picking out those situational elements which the target language selects and not striving to represent those it does not, he realizes there are situations where translation becomes partly or completely impossible, when linguistic structure is an integral part of the message or when the source culture has artefacts unknown in the target culture.

Catford is not unaware that his definition of textual equivalence poses problems. The concept of sameness of situation, as he admits (1965:52), is a difficult one, especially when very different cultures are involved. His description of how we discover textual equivalences is also dubious, although he might be less ready to accept this. Even though the process is based on a linguistic procedure called 'commutation' which works well in discovering the structural description of a language, it becomes dubious in application to translation.

Basically, it works as follows: Suppose we have a source text that says ABC and a translator tells us the equivalent should be XYZ; suppose we then commute ABC to ADC and the translation becomes XWZ; in that case, according to Catford, D and W are cross-language equivalents. This is a very dodgy notion because, as any translator knows, any number of other things might also have been said in response to the change in the source: we could have said XYA or WXY, or made no change at all. The French *Il pleut à verse* could become any of the English series *It's pouring/ tippling/siling/bucketing down* depending on the translator's whim. Catford's definition of equivalence, then, behind a façade of scientific respectability, hides a notorious vagueness and a suspect methodology.

Other criticisms made of Catford have not always been based on accurate or careful readings of his work. Larose (1989:113) claims that he decontextualizes the translation process, and yet Catford refers several times to context and uses the concept of social contextual function to suggest solutions to dialect translation, for example. Another criticism made by Larose is that Catford's theory is paralyzed at sentence level. This would certainly seem to be supported by the examples Catford uses, but the vulgar fact is that much translation does take place at that level. Larose is nonetheless right to call Catford disappointing. Much of his text on restricted translation (translating only grammar or translating the alphabet, for example) seems motivated mainly by a desire for theoretical completeness, covering all the aspects of his model, and is out of touch with what most translators have to do.

Nida and dynamic equivalence

Four years after Catford's book, Eugene Nida's even more famous attempt to deal with translation correspondence under the heading of 'dynamic equivalence' has subsequently led to denunciation rather than just criticism.

Writing in 1969 (in collaboration with Taber, who rarely gets mentioned), Nida tells us that translation theory is lagging behind translation skills and needs to catch up: "The older focus in translating was the form of the message... The new focus, however, has shifted from the form of the message to the response of the receptor" (1969:1). This means that different translations will be 'correct' for different readerships. Nida does not tell us here where this new 'spirit' comes from (we have to go back to the earlier *Toward a Science of Translating* for that) but proceeds to his famous definition ('declaration' or 'manifesto' might be better words): "Translating consists in reproducing in the receptor language the closest natural equivalent of the source-language message, first in terms of meaning and secondly in terms of style" (1969:12). He then proceeds to analyze this statement in proselytizing terms, with declarations such as "the translator must strive for equivalence rather than identity", "the best translation does not sound like a translation", and "a conscientious translator will want the closest natural equivalent". As will be seen, judgmental terms abound, and it is this normative approach, coupled with the fact that Nida works in the sensitive area of Bible translation, which has been the source of controversy.

Nida, like Martin Luther long before, wants to translate the Bible in a way that would have immediate meaning for the target-language reader, rather than as a text in which every word was God-given and therefore sacrosanct and available only to the priestly class. Somebody who has not learnt Hebrew will take the phrase *heap coals of fire on his head* as a form of torture (I certainly did), rather than meaning 'to make somebody ashamed of his behaviour' (1969:2). This concern with reader response, comprehensibility and right understanding leads Nida to make such declarations as "*To communicate effectively one must respect the genius of each language*" (1969:4, Nida's italics), and he calls on structural, psycho- and sociolinguistics to show how this can be done.

In a clear, detailed and erudite exposition, Nida and Taber show how dynamic equivalence impacts on the translation of grammatical meaning (like Catford, Nida is clear that what should be translated is grammatical function not form), referential meaning and connotative meaning. They also analyze the concept in relation to the translation of idiom, discourse structure, language variety, types of discourse and style, as well as discussing the translation process itself and the problems it poses. The result is one of the most complete and consistent discussions of translation ever produced. Despite the criticisms made of it, the book should be compulsory reading for all translators.

In his search for dynamic equivalence Nida is prepared to do things such as build in redundancy (repeating information) where a formal translation would produce a dense text, and to alter the sequence of sentences where the order of events in the original does not match real-time chronology (1964:139). Many translators of secular texts might consider that to be sound advice, but in the tradition of Biblical translation, in which St Jerome declared that "even the order of the words is a mystery", it smacks of proselytization by one church.

Another charge now made against Nida by the multiculturalists is that if we follow his injunction to preserve the genius of the target language, it will mean suppressing the Otherness of the source language and so is a form of colonialism or 'ethnocentric violence', as Venuti has it (1995:21). Such people would turn on its head Nida's declaration that the source form must be changed to preserve the meaning (1969:5) and his assertion that "The best translation does not sound like a translation" (1969:12).

The problem with the concept of dynamic equivalence does indeed appear most acutely when it produces what seem to be colonizing translations. The most notorious example is Nida's very brief mention in *Towards a Science of Translation* of the rendering of the Biblical *greet one another with a holy kiss* as *give one another a hearty handshake all around*, of which Nida says the latter "quite naturally translates" the former (1964:160). This goaded the French theorist Henri Meschonnic, who takes a mystic view of translation, into writing with some vehemence that "This automatic behavourism authorizes any kind of manipulation ... Translation becomes adaptation, with Nida's dynamic equivalence as its good conscience" (1986:77).

As with Catford, the attacks have not always been based on a careful reading of Nida. Those who have accused him of cultural imperialism have overlooked his distinction between "a linguistic translation, which is legitimate, and a cultural translation or adaptation, which is not" (1969:134), because such a cultural reinterpretation "does not take seriously the cultural outlook of the people of Biblical times" (1969:13). Nida had, in fact, already stated in his earlier book that "it is quite impossible to remove such 'foreign' objects as ... Lamb of God" (1964:167).

The problem with this is that the boundaries are not watertight. Nida does not make clear whether the 'hearty handshake' is a linguistic translation in which idiom is traded for idiom, or whether it falls under his category of "areas of tension between formal-equivalence and dynamic-equivalence translations" (1964:171). One such area consists of objects and events that exist in both source and target cultures but with a different function. In such circumstances, Nida says, one possible solution is simply to use the target-language functional equivalent, replacing, for example, 'heart' by 'liver' as an expression of the centre of emotions (1964:172), which would also justify the substitution of handshakes for kisses. A second problem with Nida's distinction, which is intended to rein in translator licence, is dealt with a few paragraphs below.

A fundamental charge made against dynamic equivalence is its essential impossibility. The Chinese scholar Qian Hu is only one in a long line to write about 'The Implausibility of Equivalent Response'. In one of a series of articles on the subject he tells us that Nida's concept is wrong because "Total compatibility between any two languages is precluded" by the very nature of language (1994:427). He points out that two speakers of the *same* language may have such different backgrounds that they will often not understand the same utterance in the same way. This is not something Nida would disagree with, and Qian Hu even quotes Nida to that effect several times. In the very first pages of *The Theory and Practice of Translation* Nida tells us, "Of course no communication, even within a single language, is ever absolute (for no two people ever understand words in exactly the same manner), and we certainly cannot expect a perfect match between languages" (1969:4-5). Few people would disagree with this. It is the cause of the misunderstandings and disputes of daily life and it follows on from what we said about languages being full of gaps in relation to one another as well as internally between individuals.

The implications for translation are certainly important, of course. If two native speakers don't even speak quite the same language as one another, how can a translator expect to react to a foreign language text like a speaker of that language? And how can we possibly begin even to know, never mind replicate, the response to a text from a culture distant in time and space? The entire first section of Steiner's *After Babel* is devoted to precisely this problem.

The importance of this is twofold. First, according to this theory of extreme subjectivity, or solipsism, any equivalent effect a translator aims for can only be an equivalence to the effect on the translator and not on the original readers. But under this theory (if you accept it) there is no way out of the prison house, so we simply plough on regardless because that is how language works.

Second, even if you do not accept this full-blown solipsism, it is obvious that languages are incommensurate in many ways. From the point of view of the intended readership, this incommensurability raises the problem of what means, if any, can be used to achieve some kind of equivalent response, and to what lengths we must go to fulfil that aim. This is a point that Gutt uses to attack Nida's theory. He explains in some detail the kind of knowledge that would be needed by a target-language audience if it is to react appropriately to a Biblical passage, then he tells us that "one would expect the theory of dynamic equivalence to provide and spell out the measures needed to achieve this" (1991:76). However, Nida's distinction between linguistic translation and cultural adaptation quoted above precludes this, according to Gutt, since the kind of explanation required is of a cultural nature, and Nida rejects cultural translation.

Gutt is in fact being disingenuous here, since on the one hand Nida does 'provide and spell out' translation measures (1964:171 et seq.) and on the other he makes a distinction between cultural translation and cultural explanation, rejecting the former but not the latter provided it is in the right place (1969:111).

The provision of any kind of explanation of the sort Gutt envisages will produce not an equivalent response but only intellectual understanding. In such cases, the theory of dynamic equivalence cannot possibly apply, unless we are prepared to turn translation into wholesale adaptation of the 'hearty handshake' variety. This means, quite simply, that there are texts or parts of texts where dynamic equivalence is not available as a tool to the translator. Conversely, there are other texts, or parts of texts, where it is available. In other words, the appropriate response to the theory of dynamic equivalence is neither unthinking acceptance nor outright rejection. It is a translation strategy to be used where appropriate, something that will be decided, not without conflict, by the wider translation culture in which each translator has a part to play, just as the wider culture will help to decide when it is appropriate to take an opera by Mozart and set it not *en una bodega* but in an American diner.

As for the practical problem raised by cultural and linguistic differences that the target audience will not understand, we dealt with these in the chapter on translation techniques and will refer to them again briefly under the heading of presupposition, so there is no need to rehearse the arguments here, but simply to say that the dividing line between translation and gloss is fuzzy rather than clear.

Successful communication beyond all manner of boundaries is a vulgar fact: linguistic groups do recognize one another beyond their individual differences; people can differentiate between a tabloid editorial, a lyrical poem and a scientific treatise, and text producers can make intelligent decisions about how much information the readership needs and how best to incorporate it. The fact that these are not rigidly definable concepts does not, in a world of chaos theory and fuzzy logic, make them invalid or inoperable.

Komissarov's sharp and fuzzy equivalence

A rather fuzzier approach to equivalence deserves mention before we wrap the topic up. It comes from eastern Europe and has the advantage of going explicitly beyond word level, which is where too much of the discussion gets stuck. We can take as our starting point a distinction made by Gak (1992:139) between three typologies of equivalence, of which only the third, stratificational equivalence, interests us here. This is equivalence defined by the linguistic level at which it takes place. There are three such levels: form, meaning, and situation (or the reality evoked, as Gak calls it), which is pretty well the same as van den Broek's hierarchical classification of equivalence into syntactic, semantic and pragmatic (1978:39). Gak says no more on the subject, but if we go back to an article by Komissarov from 1977 we find a five-term taxonomy based on the level of language at which translation equivalence is achieved. Each type of equivalence retains and adds to the features of the preceding level. They are explained below using literal translations of Komissarov's Russian examples, shown by R. (Some of his examples seem a bit odd but you'll get the idea of what he means.)

1. Equivalence can be established only at the level of the general message, with no other discernible situational, lexical or grammatical relation between source and target:

   Maybe there is some chemistry between us doesn't mix (meaning 'You and I are incompatible')
   R: *Is often that people not go together by characters*

   All that is translated in this example is the general concept of 'personal incompatibility'; the concrete metaphor has given way to general statement.

2. At this level, in addition to the communicative intention, a concrete situation is identified in both languages even though there are no matches of a lexical nature between the source language and the target language (Komissarov also says there is no syntactic match, but his example disproves that):

   He answered the telephone
   R: *He took the receiver*

   The communicative intention here is to narrate an act, and the situation identified in both languages is 'answering the phone', but there are no verbal correspondences between the two sentences other than a similar grammatical structure.

3. In addition to the communicative intention and the identification of a situation, this type preserves the general situational descriptors:

   Scrubbing makes me bad-tempered
   R: *From the washing of floors of me the character is spoilt*

   The communicative intention is expressing an attitude; the situation identified is a negative activity; and the situation is described in the same general terms (which Komissarov explains rather cryptically as 'A makes B's C contain D' for the English, and 'C which belongs to B gets D through A' for the Russian).

4. This level builds in closer semantic and syntactic relationships. Most of the source-language words have a corresponding lexical item in the target-language and the syntax is transformationally related:

I told him what I thought of her
R: *I told him my opinion of her*

5. In this type there is close parallelism between the source and the target at all levels of language:

I saw him at the theatre
R: *I saw him in theatre*

The interest of this kind of taxonomy is that it directs the translator away from the unthinking or over-anxious attempt to match word for word, which all too often produces nonsense. Sliding along the scale from type 5 to type 3 might have helped the translator who produced *After receiving strong blows in the press*, which sounds like an industrial accident but really means 'As a result of intense media criticism' or 'Following hostile press reports'. Similarly, *Today, we offer you to share this position* in an advert for a French wine purchasing company could have shifted to type 2: *Now you too can take advantage of this wonderful opportunity*. Type 1 is often a necessity in subtitling films because of the special constraints on the practice. In the film *Cible émouvante (Wild Target)*, *Comment ça: et alors, et alors?* becomes *Is that all you can say?*, while an example of Type 2 is found in the same film when the French for *get a nettle rash* is translated as *throw a tantrum*.

Of course, as with other models of equivalence, this one cannot predict the precise conditions in which each type is appropriate. As a result it may seem only a little more helpful than the old translation adage 'as literal as possible, as free as necessary'. Nor is it immune to wider considerations that would override its categories. The author of *strong blows in the press*, for example, may have been deliberately attempting to produce a foreignizing translation.

From this point of view, the various concepts and taxonomies of equivalence, hailed as our scientific guide to correct translation, turn out to have a theoretical foundation not very much firmer than the concepts of literal, faithful and free translation. But, like those concepts, the notion of equivalence and the techniques for achieving it continue to be used in the everyday language of translation because they represent translation reality. The taxonomies we have looked at are not drawn out of thin air; they are based on observations of what actually happens in translation, and different commentators at different times are finding pretty much the same things happening. Similarly, the distinction between formal and dynamic equivalence is seen in translation practice and provides a formal definition and structure for that practice. Yet it remains true that none of these concepts can operate in a vacuum. They depend on wider linguistic and cultural considerations.

6. Beyond the Word

Shveitser's judgement on Retsker was that his taxonomy of translation techniques was based too much on the lower linguistic levels of word and phrase (1987:33), a criticism echoed by Delisle (1988:44) in relation to all other such taxonomies: "One of the major weaknesses of [linguistic] theories of translation is that they have not ventured far enough beyond the word and sentence".

We shall see that this is not entirely true, but it certainly is true that adherence to the word level as a translation unit causes uncomfortable effects at the textual level, as in the sign at Berlin airport which says (unless they've changed it) *Welcome in Berlin* or the caption at the end of each episode of *Seven Cities of Gold* which read *To Follow* (a literal translation of the French original) instead of *To Be Continued*. The linguistic level at which the translation unit is set has a long and disputatious history behind it (Kelly 1979:121) and is related, as Albrecht (1973:52) amongst many others points out, to 'literal' translation (low-level translation unit) and 'free' translation (high-level units). Note, though, that although Albrecht believes that the results become less acceptable as the translator shifts the level of text segmentation down toward the word and the morpheme, he also says that such literalist translation "is not just a game for linguists; in specific circumstances it can be useful" (1973:52).

When we see somebody's translation theory criticized for being too 'word-bound', we would do well to remember that a great deal of translation takes place at this level with no adverse effects. Although it has been fashionable to claim for quite some time that 'the text is the real unit of translation', the idea has not often been properly clarified, and when Lörscher claims that "It may well be the fact that professional translators work with texts only" (1991:13) he offers no evidence to show how this might operate in reality, so that such statements sound like mere ideological posturing. The opposite point of view is put by Kade (1980:18), who says that "Texts are usually too long to be treated as a communicative unit in the transcoding process", and by Popovič (1977:13), who says "The main field where the translator's decisions take place is the level of the textual microstructure".

What professional and even novice translators actually do is relate the translation of the microlevel of words and phrases to higher textual levels of sentence and paragraph, and beyond that to such parameters as register, genre, text conventions, subject matter, and so on, in a constant dialectic. The rest of this book will look at the implications these levels have for the translator's activity.

Generative grammar

Above the level of word and phrase is the sentence. One attempt to extend the analysis of translation to this level has been to invoke generative-transformational grammar.

In the mid-1960s Noam Chomsky set the world of linguistics ablaze with two new ideas. Noting that existing linguistic theories could not easily handle certain surface features of language, he proposed a new theory, called 'generative' or 'transformational grammar', which claimed that speakers generate the more or less complicated surface structures of sentences through a series of transformations of much more basic structures called 'kernels' or 'deep structures'. Chomsky also suggested that the elements that make up the kernels are universal, existing in all languages.

The explosion of research that resulted from these ideas led to theories of such ferocious complexity that only an expert in linguistics would want to go into them. However, Nida has proposed his own far simpler version of deep structure analysis for the purposes of translation.

In his model of the translation process, Nida proposes that complex phrases or sentences in the source language should first be reduced to 'kernels' using just the four categories of Object (O) for things, Event (E) for actions, Abstraction (A) for qualities, quantities, etc., and Relation (R) for connecting words. There is nothing intrinsically wrong with these categories (they are comparable to those proposed in case grammar and semantics), although much finer classifications could certainly be made. As Andrews (1985:71) says: "There are ... many (probably infinitely many) more semantic roles that might be significant for the grammar of a language". Yet infinite taxonomies are unmanageable, so let's stick with Nida's much more practical approach.

Having analyzed our sentences into kernels, these kernels are then 'transferred' into the target language, and from there the target surface structures are arrived at by a series of transformational rules. The reason Nida suggests that translation should proceed like this has to do with Chomsky's second idea regarding universals, leading Nida to say that

> languages agree far more on the level of the kernels than on the level
> of the more elaborate structures. This means that if one can reduce
> grammatical structures to the kernel level, they can be transferred
> more readily and with a minimum of distortion. (1969:39)

In fact, Nida promptly modifies this idea of kernel-level transfer in a footnote, opening himself to the accusation that he is not working with proper transformational grammar (see Gentzler 1993:49). Yet that is not in itself a serious accusation, given that transformational-generative grammar has gone through several stages and linguists themselves have disagreed on the 'proper' model.

More important for our purposes is to see how the process might work. We shall do this by taking one of Nida's examples. The sentence *John ... [preached] a baptism of repentance for the forgiveness of sins* is analyzed as

O	E	E	R	E
John	[preached]	a baptism	of	repentance

R	E	R	E
for	the forgiveness	of	sins

Note that many words traditionally called 'nouns', which are usually defined as 'thing-words', actually turn out have the function of 'events', which have traditionally been associated with verbs, or 'doing-words'.

In order to produce complete kernels from this analysis, we must make explicit two things that are only implicit in the sentence: (i) it is *people* who receive baptism and forgiveness (they are the goal of these actions) and *people* who sin and repent (they are the subject of these actions; (ii) it is *God* who forgives (He is the subject of the action).

We are now in a position to produce our kernels:

> (1) John preached X (where X means 2 to 5 below)
> (2) John baptizes the people
> (3) The people repent
> (4) God forgives X   (where X means 5 below)
> (5) The people sin

This is simple enough. In fact, one might want to jump in and translate these 'kernels' into the target language and then work them back up to the surface. However, Nida has only said that this is the level at which 'transfer' takes place, without specifying at any point what that means. He subsequently tells us that "the kernel expressions themselves are not to be translated literally... They are only the basis for transfer" (1969:47). Again he does not say what this means, and in the later discussion of transfer and restructuring, the concept of kernels seems quietly to fade away.

It actually transpires that, after we have reduced our sentences to kernels, we must then "'back up' to the point where these kernels are carefully and properly related to each other" (1969:104) – although we are not told how to do that —, and it also transpires that in the process of our analysis we should not simply have been producing kernels but also anticipating things we know will have to happen in the target language when we restructure the kernels into surface structures. It further transpires that stylistic requirements that are not actually represented in the kernels will have to be taken into account in the restructuring process. Finally, the sole purpose of such an analysis is to identify word functions and relations; it has nothing to do with meaning, which is the subject of a different part of the translation process in Nida's scheme.

So what had seemed a simple, clear and easy-to-follow model turns out to be rather more complicated, even vague, and concerned to capture only one aspect of translation. Add to this the fact that large swathes of language can be translated without kernel analysis and we have a model which is beginning to look decidedly useless for most translation purposes. Kernel production may well help in dealing with the ambiguities produced by the highly nominalized and genitivized language of the King James bible and comparable texts, and it may be useful for trainee translators to practise as one of the forms of analysis that might occasionally be needed. But if I take a sentence at random out of a newspaper (*The squeeze on domestic demand would be at least partly offset by growth in exports* just happens to come to hand) with the aim of translating it, the effort spent in reducing it to kernels that I then do not translate seems best devoted to other matters, such as making sure that I know the technical terms for *squeeze* and *demand* in an economic context.

Shveitser: translation and rewriting rules

These objections to Nida's kernel concept are shared by Shveitser, although he largely accepts Nida's version of transformational grammar. He points out quite rightly that a phrase like *the foundations of the house*, which Nida subjected to deep structure analysis in order to explain the meaning of *of*, can be disambiguated by the context without the need for deeper analysis and can be transferred directly to the target-language surface structure (1987:47). However, Shveitser also claims that such surface transfer is possible only for related languages, whereas in translating practice it is surely the case that skilled translators have internalized their command of their second language to the point where they can go directly between the surface structures of whatever their language pair happens to be. In other words, kernel analysis is one possible tool in the translation process, but not the process itself, and not even necessarily a part of the process.

As far as Shveitser is concerned, generative grammar in its American form is inadequate for translation purposes because, at least in its early phase, it continued to ignore meaning, and so cannot account for "the mechanisms of lexical and syntactic paraphrase ... which, more complicated than grammatical transformations, are typical of language activity in general and translation in particular" (1987:51). Shveitser finds greater assistance in a Russian model which, in addition to assigning syntactic functions to words, contains deep lexis rules that assign to words information telling us (i) the equivalence substitutes for the word (synonyms, converses, derivates) and (ii) how the word collocates with others (1987:53).

A function parameter, for example, assigns *fall* to *rain* and *shine* to *sun* because that is what rain and sun do, while an inception parameter assigns *sets in* to *storm* and *breaks out* to *conflict* because that is how storms and conflicts begin. A causative parameter collocates *reduce* and *to tears* but *incite* and *to murder*, and so on.

Used in combination, such syntactic and lexical parameters allow us to maintain equivalence within an altered structure by applying rewriting rules. Thus, a conversive reformulation allows us to rewrite *many unions joined the TUC* as *the TUC counts many unions as members*, where the verb becomes its converse with reassignation of subject/object functions, while *prepare for* can become the synonymous *make preparations for* with grammatical reassignment from phrasal verb to verb phrase.

Other applications lead to greater syntactic changes, as in the pair *He subjected the patients to an examination / The patients allowed themselves to be examined by him*, in which the actants or agents reverse grammatical roles (Shveitser 1987:54).

Translators certainly do use the kind of transformations described here, as we saw in our discussion of translation techniques, and this gives some plausibility to Shveitser's view of translation as a process of paraphrase. But the rules themselves are of little use to practising translators, for three reasons.

First, Shveitser gives us a grand total of no fewer than fifty-five lexical and twenty-two syntactic rules! Although translators might profit from learning half a dozen names for translation techniques, only the most masochistic would wish to learn such a hefty apparatus as this.

Second, the rules do not all have equal status for a translator. Various localized pressures of a syntactic or stylistic nature may cause a translator to cast around for alternatives in the search for a 'better' translation, so that *the platoon was shot at* is rewritten as *the squad came under fire* (an awkward passive becomes an active and the clumsy sound combination in *was shot* disappears). But not even novice translators are going to waste time casting around for the rule that will enable them to turn *die Sonne scheint* into *the sun shines* rather than *the sun falls*.

This discrepancy arises from the fact that the generative rules Shveitser is talking about were originally intended to represent the innate language ability that a native speaker does not need to think about before speaking. A non-native speaker has acquired that knowledge in very different ways, however, and translation is not the same as speaking. A translator will focus very different levels of awareness on different elements of the text in the process of translation, pondering for hours over a small phrase that may require some conscious form of transformational manipulation, and then translating the next dozen sentences on auto-pilot because they involve only internalized linguistic routines. In other words, if transformational grammars describe how language works (and not everyone thinks they do) they do not necessarily describe how translation works.

Third, Shveitser's claim that these procedures produce equivalence of meaning in an altered structure needs to be examined carefully in each case. In any language that allows *He subjected them to examination* to be rewritten as *They allowed themselves to be examined*, there is likely to be rather more at stake than a mere reversal of roles, so Shveitser's model does not fulfil its declared aim of 'sameness in difference'.

Malone and bridge building

Also derived from generative grammar is Malone's 'bridging' technique. This takes its name from the type of bridge that can be raised and lowered between two pylons. The bridge itself will be the sentence to be translated represented in both SL and TL at some point between the deep structure and the surface structure, while the pylons symbolize the derivational rules that allow us to transform the deep structure into the surface. The idea is that we can raise our representation of the sentence closer to the surface structure or lower it towards the deep structure depending on how common the SL and TL derivations are. This overcomes the objection made against Nida, since it allows that there is little point in analyzing sentences into kernels if a direct surface translation can take place. If the surface structures of source and target languages are arrived at in the same way, no further analysis is necessary. If, however, the derivation is different, then we lower our bridge to the appropriate level of grammatical abstraction in the source language and then work our way back up the derivational rules in the target language in order to arrive at an appropriate surface structure.

Thus, the French sentence *Je tâcherais de m'y conformer* is derived from the abstract structure: JE<a> TÂCH- [+ conditional] {JE<a>CONFORM-JE<a>y} by applying rules which produce appropriate pronoun links, build in agreement between appropriate parts of the sentence, and reposition elements within the sentence.

By contrast, the English deep structure for the translation of this sentence, which is: I <a> would try {I<a>ACCOMMODATE I<a>to them}, requires only two rules: one to handle the pronouns and the other to produce an appropriate verb form to give the surface structure *I would try to accommodate myself to them* (Malone 1988:147). The fact that only part of the English sentence is represented in deep structure form with the first part (*I would try*) already in its surface structure is presumably intended to demonstrate Malone's notion that bridge technique need only be applied when the differences between source-language and target-language derivations are great enough to justify the work.

The derivation rules needed to go from deep to surface structure are taken from standard transformational grammar. We mention only two taken at random to convey the flavour of the process:

- *Equi* deletes links in a coreference chain: the not impossible English sentence *He wants he should do this himself* would become *He wants to do this himself*;
- *Rais* takes an element in the subordinate clause and raises it into the main clause: compare *What I want is that you shut up* with *I want you to shut up*.

As with Shveitser, the different transformational rules have different status when it comes to translation (as opposed to generating sentences in one's native language). Thus, the use of a *RelPro* rule to insert a relative pronoun can be a deliberate translator choice for running short sentences into a longer sentence, possibly for stylistic reasons, but many of the rest do not represent translator choice. For example, the rule which positions object pronouns is a grammatical imposition in many languages, what Vinay and Darbelnet called a 'servitude', and as such a translator has no choice but to apply them.

Many commentators have pointed out that the processes described by Nida, Shveitser and Malone, among others, almost certainly have little to do with what goes on in the heads of actual translators. These models are based on the assumption that the translation process consists of three phases: analysis into deep grammar and meaning, mental transfer from the source language to the target language (sometimes via some mysterious interlanguage called a *tertium comparationis*), and restructuring to produce an acceptable text (Nida 1969:33), although none of these theorists are necessarily claiming that the phases occur separately one after the other.

These models are heavily marked by information theory and computer modelling approaches with their concepts of input, treatment, and output. As Lörscher (1991:17) points out, such process models of translation are purely logical constructs with no proven psychological reality. Where translators do bother to analyze a text (and whole segments of texts can be translated without such conscious work), their analyses are far more likely to take the form of discursive explanations to themselves of what they think the text is about rather than careful reduction to kernels and reassembly as surface structures. Lörscher's research suggests that translators actually use the minimax principle: they keep the mental burden as low as possible by making use of deeper, more abstract, and therefore more difficult processing levels only when higher-level processing has failed (Lörscher 1991:267). We shall have more to say about this in the section on psycholinguistics.

On the whole, the grammar of deep structure and transformational rules, dramatic as its impact may have been on linguistics, would seem to have little to offer to the study of translation. Not only does it not offer any real insight into translation, it is, as Gentzler (1993:50) rightly says, actually divorced from real translation problems: "from contemporary neologisms to archaisms, from proper nouns to metaphors, from high registers to dialects and 'mistakes' and all those knotty problems that make translation both impossible and fascinating".

Another aspect of meaning commonly attributed to whole sentences rather than words concerns the things that sentences imply or presuppose. Since these are often linked to language in use, we shall leave consideration of this area of semantics to the chapter on pragmatics. Our next task, however, will be to look at the linguistics of what happens beyond the level of the sentence in the realm of context and register.

7. Beyond the Sentence: Context and Register

Context

One of the most frequent injunctions in translation is to 'look at the context', and one reason transformational grammar has so little to offer translation is its refusal to do precisely that (Faiss 1973:78). Most words entered in the mono- and bilingual dictionary have multiple meanings; the one-to-many equivalence relation. Only by looking at the company a word keeps can we find out which meaning is to be activated in a specific instance. *She won the butterfly* might mean that some lucky woman drew the winning ticket for a lepidoptera, but could mean she won a swimming race. We need the context to tell us. This seems to be such an obvious fact that it may come as some surprise to find that the concept of context is not unproblematic in linguistics (and is even rejected in deconstructionist analyses on the grounds that every word always contains traces of all its meanings).

According to Leech (1981:61ff) the notion of context emerged as an attempt to remove language from the purely mental sphere, amenable only to unreliable introspection, and put it in a perspective that would allow scientific observation. This perspective was the concrete situation in which the language was being used and the things being done with language in that situation: buying a train ticket, being arrested by the police ...

This use of the word 'context' is no longer quite the same as it was in the preceding paragraph, where it meant literally 'the text that goes around the text we are looking at'. To make this clear, some writers refer to the wider meaning of context as 'the context of situation' and the narrower meaning as 'co-text'. Holz-Mänttäri's *Handlungstheorie* reminds us that the act of translation also has its own institutional context while Vermeer's concept of *Skopostheorie* reminds us that a translation has to function in a context different from that of the source text (see Christiane Nord in this series).

The attractiveness of the concept of context seems obvious. If it works, it allows us to describe the linguistic behaviour of a given situation in a scientific way, to find out how other languages handle the context in question, and to translate accordingly, using just the form of words we desperately need to translate our source text. Just as we know without a shadow of doubt that in a specific situation *è pericoloso sporgersi* equals (very precisely) *do not lean out of the window* (and not *it is dangerous to lean out*) and *défense d'entrer* equals (rather less precisely) *no entry* (and not *forbidden to enter*), so we might hope to find the precise contextual parameters that tell us how to translate, without a shadow of a doubt, *Longtemps je me suis couché de bonne heure* or *Four score years ago and ten.*

You might, for example, be translating a text in which *Mr and Mrs Smith go to the grocers* (anything is possible). All you have to do, in order to translate this, is to match it with the words that would be used in that very same grocery-buying situation in the target culture, taking care only to allow for the fact that foreigners eat some funny things (the English eat parsnips when every good French person knows they are meant for pig feed).

The problem, as Leech says, is that such situations are 'primitive' (1981:64). As long as the parties concerned confine themselves as good capitalists to the business of buying and selling groceries using the appropriate set phrases that regulate such a transaction, we have a situation that just might possibly be described with the scientific accuracy envisaged by the contextualists. But if Mr Smith grows prize cucumbers and has strict, not to say manic, ideas on the subject, he might engage the grocer in a discussion that is purely tangential to or even has nothing to do with the situation in hand, and which, from the linguistic point of view, will require the notion of context to be widened to take in the theory and practice of horticulture as well as the art of polemic in a public place.

This, according to Leech (1981:64), is precisely what happened with contextualism. The notion of context was diluted to the point where it became too abstract to permit the scientific descriptions which had been its main purpose.

Eggins (1994:8) is able to say very precisely that in the context of a recipe book you would not expect to find such sentences as *Perhaps you should maybe mix the eggs and milk for about two minutes or so*, since the writing of recipes is a rigidly controlled genre, but she would have far more difficulty saying precisely what kind of language you might or might not find in an article on garden gnomes or Kevin Bacon.

Although the concept of context can be used to (i) resolve ambiguity, (ii) provide referents for words like *this* and *then*, and (iii) supply information that makes sense of elliptical utterances, Leech demonstrates quite easily that there can be no such thing as an exhaustive scientific description of a given context, and that the term may have some use in pragmatics but has none in semantics.

Of course, rejecting context on scientific-linguistic grounds does not render the concept unusable. Just as terms such as 'literal' and 'free' translation and 'equivalence' continue to be used by translators even though there is no accepted 'scientific' definition of them, so translators continue to refer to context. As is so often the case, translation has to rely on fuzzy concepts that are not amenable to scientific definition but which can be made workable for practical purposes. The mystery, perhaps, is why theorists are so determined to defuzz the discipline.

One simple exercise to demonstrate the practical applicability of context would be to take a sentence such as the French *Je vais à l'école* and ask in what contexts the following translations would be appropriate: *I go to school, I'm going to school, I'm going to the school* and *I'm driving to college*, together with any others you can think of (Pergnier 1993:51-52).

Context can, at least for some of its dimensions, be approached from two directions: first, from the point of view of 'register', the specification of the elements of the communicative event, its participants and parameters, and second, from the point of view of 'scenes-and-frames', which is a kind of updated version of contextualism.

Communicative event and register

Journalists used to be, probably still are, taught that the first paragraph of their article should give the answers to 'Who, what, when, where, and why'. These are the basic elements of any situation. According to Nord (1991:36), who gives a potted history of this question list all the way back, would you believe, to Hermagoras of Temnos (2 BCE!), the complete list should be:

> *Who* transmits
> *to whom*
> *what for*
> *by which medium*
> *where*
> *when*
> *why*
> > a text
> *with what function?*
>
> *On what subject matter*
> > do they say
> *what*
> *(what not?)*
> *in what order*
> *using which non-verbal elements*
> *in which words*
> *in what kind of sentences*
> *in which tone*
> *to what effect?*

Nord has attempted to put the extratextual factors in the first paragraph and the intratextual factors in the second. This list is encapsulated quite neatly in the register model of text.

Register

At the centre of language is variability. We don't all speak in exactly the same way all the time. Language varies in different contexts and situations of use. This is accounted for in linguistics by 'register analysis'. As always in linguistics, there is no one standard presentation of the register model, but the fundamentals are the same. The two main parameters that cause language to vary are language user and language use, and both parameters can be described in terms of a set of sub-parameters. Changes in any of these will produce changes in the language used.

Register and language user

Language users can be described by the place they occupy in:

- time (what age do/did they live in?)
- space (what region do/did they come from?)
- society (what social class do/did they belong to?)

From a purely linguistic point of view these parameters seem unexceptional. From other points of view they become problematic, as we shall see. However, the first sub-parameter (time) would seem to be uncontroversial. Writers and translators live in a certain era and the language they use will be date-stamped for that era, with words that subsequently disappear or change meaning, grammatical structures that later fall out of use, even different spelling. The real question for translation is quite simply this: Should the translation of an earlier text be written in the modern target language or an earlier version of it? Should Dostoevsky be translated into the English of Dickens?

In the vast majority of cases the answer is no and this parameter has no influence on translation. Unless a translator has taken the immense trouble to learn the earlier form of the language, the result will almost certainly be risible pastiche. The larger the temporal gap to be bridged, the more alien such a translation becomes to its readers, who might just as well learn the foreign language and enjoy the original.

One writer who has attracted this sort of attention is the medieval Italian author Dante, whose *Divine Comedy* was translated into medieval French in the nineteenth century and an invented medieval German in the twentieth century, even though Dante's medieval Italian is far less different from modern Italian than medieval French or German is from modern French or German. The result, as Zimmer (1981:135) says, is little more than an intellectual game.

There are cases, usually but not only in literary translation, however, where a part of the original text will make use of different historical stages of the language: the discovery of an ancient manuscript or an imagined future language, for example. In such cases a holistic or illusionistic approach to translation comes into its own. Zimmer (1981:133) gives the example of a novel by Thomas Mann which contains a passage written in 'archaic' German. The French translator has not attempted to use authentic archaic French, preferring simply to take whatever opportunities arise to use older forms of spelling and the occasional archaic word, giving a form of French that has never actually existed but which gives the illusion of being plausibly dated for modern readers.

There are two other main ways in which the temporally marked aspect of language influences translation. The first is the need to prepare new translations when existing ones are perceived to be out of touch with the modern state of the language, although economic reasons may mean that this process applies only to 'classic' texts. The second is the desire to avoid new translations because of the perceived classic status of an existing translation or the belief that a translation close in time to the original is likely to be a better representation of the language of the original.

The other two parameters defining language user, region and social class, seem superficially uncontroversial but prove not to be. If all or part of a source text is written in a regional language, the translator may want to reflect that in the translation. We shall return to this point under the heading of sociolinguistics, where we will see that dialect translation is by no means as simple and straightforward as one might think, especially since it often relates to questions of status and repression.

The last parameter (social class) may have seemed uncontroversial when the concept of register was first elaborated, and in many language communities it still is. The idea that the 'unmarked' register, in other words the accepted standard, should be the language of the 'educated middle classes' was accepted without a murmur of protest at a time when the sociolinguist Bernstein was able to compare what seemed to be the richness and diversity of the 'extended' language code used by the educated bourgeoisie with the impoverished nature of the 'restricted' code of the working classes. Since then, just as the so-called poverty of the restricted codes has come under attack, so too has the notion of a middle-class white norm also been subjected to (largely unsuccessful) assault.

Ideological considerations also influence this parameter in translation. The ideology of the target culture may not permit the use of anything other than the standard dialect, in which case suppression will be the translation strategy adopted. Alternatively, a source text written in the standard language may be translated into a non-standard language (we shall see some examples in the chapter on sociolinguistics). In other cases, the translator will be allowed and will try to represent variations in social class markers in the text to be translated. Translators should therefore be able to recognize these markers and be able to reproduce them as appropriate in the target language.

Neither of these tasks is as easy as it sounds, since the translator may have had no exposure to different varieties of the foreign source language, while in the native target language translators may be able to recognize varieties, but may not be able to produce them. We can all recognize the different regional pronunciations of our own country but we cannot all imitate them, and the same is true of written registers. The most common type of translator may well by the third type in Levý's tripartite division (1969:63): those who only ever use their own 'idiolect', their own individual and specific way of using language. We shall see an example of this at the end of the section on function in translation.

Register and language use

The 'language user' was the first parameter of register description. The second is 'language use'. Just as the language user was defined by three sub-parameters of place, time and status, so now it is customary to describe language use in terms also of three sub-parameters: tenor, mode and domain. Of these three sub-parameters, the first two can be defined quite precisely, while the third seems to be a more slippery concept.

'Tenor' is used to describe the relationship of text producer to text receiver, as reflected, for example, in the difference between *Please place in the receptacle provided* and *Bob it in the bin*, between *Bitte gehen Sie weg* and *Hau ab*, between *Ayez l'obligeance de quitter ma présence l* and *Foutez-moi le camp d'ici*. A text will usually have an abundance of lexical, grammatical and syntactic markers to show the degree of formality, distance and politeness between the sender and the receiver, a degree which may vary from the formal or even frozen language of officialese to the most intimate of personal talk.

What actually determines this degree of distance and consequent formality may be social status (the first letter I got from my university in England began 'Dear Fawcett') or the authority that comes with knowledge ("The existence of mediation does not entail the existence of either Kuhnian paradigms or Foucauldian epistemes" (Benjamin 1989:32) – no, I don't know what it means either). But distance can also be decided by something as simple as available space: the standard phrase on branded medicine containers, *If symptoms persist consult your doctor*, is often replaced nowadays where space allows by the friendlier, more informal but slightly longer *If symptoms do not go away, talk to your doctor about it.*

The second sub-parameter of language use is 'mode' or 'channel'. At its simplest, this is the choice between speaking and writing. A couple who have fallen out and who are not on speaking terms may communicate through notes stuck to the fridge door, and the tone is apt to be icy (*I shall return home at 5 p.m.* rather than *Back at 5*). Speaking and writing can be done alone (monologue) or with other people (dialogue). This parameter can become very complex, however, because within both speaking and writing there will be many variations on the main theme. We can chat informally to friends supplementing our words with a whole array of body language, or be interviewed formally by a customs officer over certain undeclared items. We can write informally in a diary with a plethora of exclamation marks, underlinings and coloured inks, or make a formal typed complaint to somebody in authority. At stake, in addition to the dimension of formality deriving from tenor, will be such things as the balance between explicit and implicit information, the degree of planning involved, and the carefulness or otherwise of the structure of the message.

Some languages have clearly demarcated spoken and written forms, whereas other languages have more fluid frontiers which can be a source of pitfalls. A French academic colleague once refused to translate a newspaper headline referring to *kids* by the equivalent *gosses* because in his opinion that word belonged only to informal spoken language.

The more fluid the borderline between what counts as purely spoken and what is allowed in writing, the more difficult decisions become, especially when we take account of language changing over time. Can teachers of translation into English continue to boldly reject split infinitives or refuse split phrasal verbs that they will not put up with? The classic example of this is French, where the complexity of the written language in relation to the spoken language led the Ministry of Education to issue regularly revised editions of 'dispensations', lists of 'mistakes' that teachers were no longer to mark wrong.

For most translators other than interpreters the problem of translating spoken language does not arise. Although the language of theatre, when intended for performance, has to be translated in a way that makes it speakable by the players, the 'speech' we are dealing with has been filtered through the writing system and tends to be a conventionalized representation rather than the real thing (verbatim transcriptions of real spoken language make for tedious reading). This is why the English translator John London

(1990:161) discovered with surprise that the actors often replaced his own translation by lines that he himself considered to be unidiomatic.

In film dubbing also the constraints of synchronization may override the need to represent the spokenness of the language, while one area of translation where the difference between the written and spoken language may be shown up quite cruelly is in the subtitling of films, where constraints of space force the use of often formal structures of a kind not found in the spoken language in its current form. One of the subtitles in the Filipino film *Manila: In the Claws of Darkness* is *You see nothing but my pate*, a sentence you are unlikely to hear in spoken English.

For most translators the constraints of mode will require control of the very wide range of written expressions appropriate to the third parameter of language use, namely 'domain', also called 'field' or 'province'.

The meaning of this parameter is not as clear as the previous two. Hatim and Mason say "field is not the same as subject matter" (1990a:48), but Bell says "in a very much broader sense, domain can refer to ... family, friendship, education and so forth" (1991:191), which sounds very much like subject matter. Crystal and Davy (1969:73) say that 'province' should not be identified with subject matter, even though they define province as the language of advertising, the language of public worship, etc., which also sounds very much like subject matter.

In the brief examples they give, Hatim and Mason (1990a:52-53) describe the 'field' of four different extracts as follows:

i   arousing interest in the topic
ii   American domestic policy and international current affairs
iii news reporting
iv   assessing current affairs (investigative journalism)

These seem to be very different kinds of thing: (i) is a text function; (ii) is subject matter; (iii) is either a professional activity or a text type; (iv) is a combination of text function, subject matter, and professional activity or text type.

Part of the problem in defining this parameter is that in practice all of the parameters of register are imbricated in one another. The language of a text may be formal not just because of tenor (the writer maintains distance from the reader) but also because of mode (written language tends to be more formal than spoken) and province (we don't often write in slang about nuclear physics). The amount of information included may not just be a function of using the written mode, which has to find ways of providing information that in conversation would be conveyed by context and body language, but also because we might choose to treat people we are speaking to as if they were stupid and needed things spelling out (in a loud voice).

For all practical purposes, this parameter seems to be a combination of subject matter, in so far as it influences choice of lexis, and genre or format of delivery in so far as it influences such parameters as formality, complexity and presentational modes. This would mean the important dimension of participation could be subsumed just as much under 'province' as under its normal location with 'tenor'. Participation concerns the extent to which the text producer attempts to 'involve' the reader in the text in some way. Authors can try to make the text receiver participate more closely in the communicative event either because they want to get close to them or show friendliness (tenor), or because the textual conventions require it (province). The anonymous author of a pantomime wants the audience to shout 'Watch out, he's behind you!' not as a mark of personal closeness with the audience but because the genre is dead without it.

Register in practice

One of the earliest applications of the concept of register to translation was provided by House, who demonstrated its use in assessing the quality of a translation. Although the model she uses is slightly different from the one outlined above, it covers all the same parameters and adds to it the concept of 'social role relationship' (1977:45) which, in addition to the equality-power dimension, also includes the related concept of positional role versus situational role. Our positional role, what we do in life, will affect the way we use language. House quotes such 'high-status' examples as teacher or priest, but people such as plumbers and carpenters will also use language dictated by their position in life, and that language will include variations depending on whether the addressee is the customer, the supplier or the apprentice. The situational role is more transient: the plumber at school on parents' night, or the teacher having a tooth removed.

In addition to register, House draws on the concept of text function. We shall look at this notion in more detail in a later section. All we need to know here is that House takes the source text and analyzes each of the register parameters to see how they contribute to conveying information (province) and to building a relationship between author and reader (tenor). She then analyzes the target version and provides a text profile of the quality of the translation not just on the basis of the traditional criterion of a semantico-grammatical mismatch (the meaning is wrong or the target-language norms are violated) but by the degree of register match or mismatch, a dimension that was either missing or inadequately developed in earlier models of translation quality assessment.

This is clearly a good idea, but it is rendered somewhat murky by House's decision to refer to semantico-grammatical mistakes as 'overtly erroneous errors' and register mistakes as 'covertly erroneous errors', which is just the kind of jargon translators can do without.

House subjects a number of text types to register analysis. Here we shall look at just one, because this particular analysis has been the subject of criticism by Gutt in his attempt to prove that translation theory needs none of the traditional apparatus of function, equivalence and so forth (we shall analyze his position in a later section).

The text is taken from a travel brochure about the town of Nuremberg. The medium is simple written-to-be-read, with no spoken language markers (it is important in register analysis to note things that are not there, as well as those that are). The text is mainly a monologue (no second person pronouns) with some attempts at dialogue (one use of *we*, some structures and lexis implying an invitation to come and see the town). The relationship between author and reader is mainly impersonal (the author is anonymous, the readership is not some specific social group) but the text tries to flatter the reader by referring to landmarks in the town by name alone, without further explanation, so supposing the reader is a person of knowledge. The tenor of the text is partly formal, using some older or archaic structures and vocabulary. The province is marked by the clichéd hyperbole and 'poetic' language typical of holiday brochures. House's analysis is much longer than this, but the above notes should give an idea of the process.

In her evaluation of the translation House makes two main points, which we shall simply summarize here without the detailed supporting proof she supplies: (i) that the translation fails to flatter the reader at crucial points, and (ii) that it fails to match the pseudo-poetic exaggeration and pretension typical of travel advertising. The first of these points is not seen as an error, since an English-speaking audience cannot be expected to understand the references to the cultural artefacts and so needs the explanations built in by the translator, even though this loses the element of flattery. The second item, loss of pretension, is seen as a 'covertly erroneous error' because the register dimension could have been respected in translation.

Gutt (1991:46-49) believes both of these conclusions are faulty. His criticism is important for translation, even if you don't accept it, because it concerns a question of vital importance for translators: How closely will the reader read the text and can we know what the effect of the text will be on the reader?

In relation to the social role relationship of flattery, Gutt doubts first whether the author of the German original deliberately intended to flatter their audience, and second whether the German audience actually would have felt flattered anyway. This relates both to the 'intentional fallacy', the false belief that an authorial intention can be recovered from a text, and to the reception-theory claim that effects on a readership can be gauged. The debate on whether intention and effect can be known is by no means over. Literary critics who, in the 1980s, fervently proclaimed the 'death of the author', who they saw as a linguistico-social construct rather than a person speaking in his or her own voice, returned in the 1990s to searching through authors' work for clues to their lives. Interested readers will find a useful introduction with further reading in the first two chapters of *Translating Poetic Discourse* by Myriam Diaz-Diocaretz (1985).

But even if flattery in the Nuremberg travel brochure was intended by the German author and received by the German audience, then surely, Gutt argues, the translator could have reacted to loss of flattery in the English version by the use of compensation: they could have built in forms of flattery to ensure overall functional equivalence of the translation with the original. This argument allows Gutt to deploy the *reductio ad absurdum* of suggesting that the translator should maintain a strict mathematical flattery count or test the translation for flattery effect on a sample audience. However, there are two flaws in Gutt's argument. First, the failure of an individual translator to behave in a certain way does not invalidate the model that analyzes that behaviour. Second, compensation is not some sort of neutral translation technique to be deployed like universal filler whenever a crack appears in the wall of translation. It is a disruptive move that has ideological overtones and is for that reason not used by all translators and need not therefore be predicted by any translation model.

On the second of House's points, that of the translation failing to match the pseudo-poetry of the original, Gutt's criticism is again both apposite and dubious. He points out that the target language may not accept pretension and exaggeration in a text of this type, and that the translation should not therefore attempt a match on this dimension. This is certainly true, and indeed he is obliged to quote House herself to precisely that effect, so his only real criticism comes down to suggesting that House should have laid greater emphasis than she does on the culture-bound nature of register.

Nonetheless, Gutt's overall criticism remains correct: Even if we accept that a translation has to be functionally equivalent to the original (which is not House's position, since, as we shall see below, she accepts the existence of function-altering translation), the model is insufficiently predictive in spelling out what this means in practice, which is precisely the same criticism we have noted in relation to the application of translation techniques.

These rather abstract considerations should not be allowed to hide the considerable importance of the linguistic concepts behind register analysis, especially for translators who are not content to approach their task haphazardly in the hope that 'it'll be all right on the night', but who prefer to come to the task in some planned kind of way. From this point of view register analysis serves several important purposes.

First, all translators should be able to perform a register analysis for two reasons: (i) in order to have an understanding of the text they are translating which goes beyond the simple level of denotation and allows them to choose the appropriate register in the target language, and (ii) so that when they are required to tackle new subject matters they can produce their own analysis of the registers available for that subject in both the source and target languages.

This is important because trainee translators have a tendency to shift registers without reason, like the student who alternated colloquialisms such as *drugged up to the eyeballs* with formal syntax like *takes not the slightest interest*, and formal vocabulary such as *evince a studied vulgarity* with informal phrases such as *comes across as*, even though the original text was written in a uniform register. Another student allowed spoken language to erupt into formal written language in the sentence *the corporation cynically stated that the pesticides, I quote, 'had been used incorrectly'*. Similarly, attention to register might have prompted a search for a more formal phrase to replace the last three words in *comparing anthropophagy to the cravings of pregnant women makes us laugh*.

Second, the assumption is that the registers appropriate in a given situation will vary between languages, as both Gutt and House point out. As a corollary, register shifts would have to occur in the process of translation. Sadly, however, very little comparative work seems to have been done in this field. This is not really surprising given the theoretical difficulties involved. If we try to draw conclusions from source texts and their translations we run the risk of methodological unsoundness since the translations may be faulty. If we work with parallel texts in bilingual publications such as those put out by the United Nations or by the Aéroport de Paris, we have no guarantee that the independently working authors were aiming at the same register. Comparing a UNESCO report on drugs written in French, German and English, we find differences such as the following:

- experience seems to demonstrate that it is unrealistic
- l'expérience semble montrer que c'est là un objectif chimérique
- doch zeigt die Erfahrung, daß dies eine völlig unzulängliche Aufforderung ist

or again:

- much has happened
- beaucoup de chemin a été parcouru
- es ist viel Zeit vergangen

Each language uses somewhat different verbal strategies which impact on textual tone (tenor). But without detailed and voluminous analysis we cannot say whether these strategies are specific to the translators involved or part of a consistent register difference in this style of report.

Similarly, in a 1991 edition of the bilingual *Austria Today*, where the German says 'borrow' (i.e. steal) a car for a 'merry trip', the English says *bands of teenagers steal automobiles and race them against each other on public roads. It is almost a mass 'sport' in some countries. Even a quiet personal 'borrowing' of somebody else's vehicle for a quick 'tour'*.... Is this because the author believes the English register should be more sensational, or because they have a somewhat hysterical personality? Whatever the case, there is little solid data for translators to go on, other than their own experience.

We have suggested above that French is less ready to mix language levels than English. Sa'Adeddin (1990:32) points to the insincerity and effusiveness that would result from the close translation of an Arabic text, where the original Arabic would appear dull and arrogant without the material that causes problems in translation. Neubert (1977:55) also reports that Anglo-American newspapers use a wider range of registers than their Russian or German counterparts, which has two consequences: in translating from English into Russian or German there should be a general raising and neutralizing of marked Anglo-American styles, while those translating in the opposite direction will have the more difficult task of building in greater stylistic variation. The example given by Neubert illustrates the problem. If you were translating from German into English the headline *EWG-Manipulation, Skandal um heimliche Gelder*, how likely are you to think of *EEC Brainwash: Row Over Cash*? Working in the opposite direction should be easier because the translation becomes more of an explanation, using abstract hypernyms rather than the English concrete hyponyms.

8. Text Structure

In our section 'Beyond the word' we looked at sentence meaning in relation to generative grammar, which is one approach to meaning created by the grammatical structure of the sentence and the functions of its components. Another type of sentence meaning is created by its conceptual structure which is dealt with in linguistics under the heading of 'theme-rheme' organization or 'functional sentence perspective'. Larger textual structures are dealt with under the headings of 'cohesion' (grammatical and lexical linkage) and 'coherence' (conceptual linkage). Here we shall look at all of these concepts.

Theme/rheme and functional sentence perspective

The semantic organization of the sentence or clause into two parts, the 'theme' (what we are talking about) and the 'rheme' (what we say about the theme), would seem to be a matter of common sense. Nothing could be further from the truth. Getting into the subject can be like bounding onto a holiday beach and then wishing you'd been more attentive to the sign that said 'Danger: Quicksand'.

The 'standard' approach is to call whatever comes in first position in the sentence the theme. Whatever follows that is the rheme. Themes are then classified (Eggins 1994:274ff) according to the nature of the linguistic item in first position. These will be different for different sentence types. Deviations from the norm are then called 'marked theme'. This in itself might seem unobjectionable. Matters become complicated when one tries to explain the function of such positioning, given that word order is highly regulated in some languages and very loose in others.

East European linguists, who did much of the early work on theme and rheme, wanted to know the difference between sentences such as the Russian *Anna liubit Ivana* ('Ann loves John') with the object in its 'normal' position after the verb and *Ivana liubit Anna* ('Ann loves John') with the object in an 'abnormal' position at the front of the sentence. The answer, according to Comrie (1979), is found by asking what question each sentence might be a reply to. In the first case, it is 'Who does Ann love?' and in the second 'Who loves John?'

The first question already gives the name Ann, so when the question is answered, this 'old' information is got out of the way by putting it first, leaving the tasty new information tantalizingly to the end: 'Ann loves John'. In other words, we follow the information pattern old-to-new. When the question is 'Who loves John?', we can do the same thing in Russian. We can put the old information (John) first and the new information (Ann) second, because the word ending tells us that *Ivana* is the object of love and *Anna* its source.

If we wanted to get the same information flow in English, and discussions of the subject in translation theory tend to assert that we do, then we might have to use a variety of what are actually quite difficult and unusual structures such as the passive (*John is loved by Ann*) or so-called clefted structures involving splitting devices such as *It is X who ...* or *What X did was to ....* Such might have been the intention of the student who translated a German inversion into the clefted structure *On October 7 1949, there was founded the German Democratic Republic*, but this is really just a bad translation using a rather antiquated structure.

However, this notion of 'new' versus 'old' (or 'given' as it is also called) is rather less obvious than it appears. As Diller and Kornelius (1978:50-51) point out, deciding precisely what is new information in a sentence by looking at a statement (*Cain kills Abel*) and asking a question (*Who does Cain kill?*) falls foul of a simple fact: we could also have asked *What does Cain do to Abel?*, *What does Cain do?*, or *Who kills Abel?*. If a language has a fixed word order system, the new information called for by these different questions cannot necessarily be signalled by simply positioning it toward the end of the clause. Sentences like *John is loved by Ann* or *It is by Ann that John is loved* as a device for getting new information into rheme position may be popular in linguistic textbooks but the average English speaker (or writer) rarely resorts to them (the word processor used to write this book issues stern warnings whenever it finds them). In such languages, other means exist to indicate new information. In English, stress patterns can be used, and not simply in speaking. It is a fairly common experience for an English person to have to re-read a written sentence because their first mental representation of the stress pattern was wrong.

The very first words of a text are in theme position but are totally new to us in relation to that particular text. Leonora Cherniakhovksaia (1977:89) quotes two Russian sentences (given here in literal translation) that are of apparently similar structure:

- In Armenia was born the new production of Britten
- On the streets of the capital of Armenia appeared posters

but which were translated differently into English as:

- While in Armenia, Britten composed ...
- Posters ... appeared in the streets of Armenia's capital.

The explanation Cherniakhovksaia gives is that in the first sentence *In Armenia* is not new information (the sentence does not come from the beginning of the text) but the second half is. Both languages handle this information structure in the same way, from old to new. In the second sentence, both parts of the sentence are new information because it's the first sentence in the text. In this situation, Russian creates a hierarchy of importance for the new information and sends the most important to rheme position. But in English the information flow is decided by the fixed grammatical structure (it would be possible but very clumsy to send 'posters' to end-position). Cherniakhovskaia (1977:90) uses theme-rheme theory to explain why an initial adverbial phrase in Russian sentences is usually transformed into grammatical subject in English: the Russian *In the room set in deathly silence* becomes English *The room turned deathly silent* and *To this period belong Lissitsky's first works* becomes English *This period saw Lissitsky's first works*.

Theme-rheme has also been explained as Topic-Comment. Theme is what we are talking about (topic) and rheme is what we are saying about it (comment). This is why, in Eggins's account, the theme part of the sentence is not just the first word or phrase but extends to include the first properly 'topical' item. A news bulletin might begin with something like *Today, in New York, three armed men seized hostages* …. (German news bulletins follow a similar structure: *Bonn: der Bundeskanzler* ….) Clearly, the initial adverbial phrases in this example are not the topic of the utterance, which is 'three armed men', so we need to explain why this item is not the very first in the sentence. The standard account acknowledges the 'real' topic and includes it in the theme but gives the theme a different name (topical, interpersonal, textual) depending on what linguistic item comes first. This is a rather mechanical solution. In our example, the fronting of the adverbial phrases may not be a thematizing device, but may instead serve one of two quite different pragmatic purposes: getting relevant but non-essential details out of the way or dramatizing the event by stage-setting.

Hawkins (1986:47) acknowledges that the information structure of the sentence is "a more subtle phenomenon" than imagined, and he points out that "there appear to be other pragmatic functions performed by word order variants which (if they have been discussed at all) have been lumped together under a simplifying Theme-Rheme rubric". So rather than seeing sentence structure simply in terms of theme-rheme, given-new or topic-comment, translators need to be aware of a hierarchy of semantic weighting of information in and between sentences and the function it serves. They need to know what the 'normal' order of words is, in so far as there is one, and then to assess the meaning of any changes to that, since in language we convey meaning by doing what is less expected.

What, for example, might be the differences, in terms of stress, focus, contrast or even text type, between:

> The cat sat on the mat
> On the mat sat the cat
> Sat the cat on the mat

where the first is unmarked and the others marked? The most likely explanation of the second is that it is part of a presentational sequence aiming for narrative climax (*on the floor was a mat and on the mat sat the cat*), which is why this sequence is typical of such text types as telling jokes or stories in English. The third example (*sat the cat on the mat*) might be interpreted as poetic (also text type). Whatever the explanation, only the context will tell us. And what the translator needs to know is how the target language achieves the effect in question.

We have talked above of standard and marked theme positions. But what is standard and marked varies between languages. This difference creates a small problem with the second sentence in the following extract from an advert translated from French for publication in an English newspaper: *You surely know or can imagine how exciting is the search [for good wines]. In France, we do this search for our customers.* Leaving aside the incongruity of saying the search is exciting and then offering to deprive customers of that excitement, you might want to ask yourself, as an exercise in assessing differential weighting within a sentence, why a better translation would have been something like *Our company already carries out this search on behalf of our customers over in France.*

Theme distribution over a longer stretch of text than the clause or sentence can turn the unmarked into the marked. In the German travel brochure analysed by House, which we discussed under register, every paragraph except the first starts with the theme *Nuremberg*. This density of repetition takes an unmarked thematic structure and makes it marked (a feature which the translator failed to reflect). Something similar happens in the following French text (presented here in literal translation and in reduced form to make the point more clearly): *Today, mad cow disease ... Yesterday, contaminated blood. Before yesterday Minamata disease. Tomorrow other evils or threats ... And then there will be yet more threats ...*

Clearly, the fronting of an adverb of time, fairly normal and therefore unmarked in French, becomes marked through the process of parallelism in which the same grammatical class recurs several times throughout the text segment in the same place but with a different content. This takes us into the subject of cohesion, which we discuss below. But before we come to that subject, the French text raises several points of importance for translation and will round off our discussion of theme-rheme.

First, the French text can be translated into English without disrupting the theme order, but there are languages where this may not be the case. The assumption is that not all languages organize theme-rheme in the same way, and indeed may not even have a theme-rheme structure. However, reservations of this kind tend to be couched in tentative language. Thus there is a 'suggestion' (Baker 1992:133) that Dutch may find fronted adverbs of time quite unusual, making a translation of our French text problematic. James (1980:115-6) quotes 'highly tentative' research suggesting that French, but not English, can structure paragraphs in such a way that the rheme of each sentence remains constant, as in *Cats eat rats. Dogs eat rats. Snakes eat rats.* Hawkins quotes research, later queried, suggesting that the unmarked order of German complements (Indirect Object+Direct Object) can only be inverted, become marked, provided the pattern of Theme+Rheme is followed.

Second, although the French text thematizes time, it jumps around in the temporal sequence. It might be the case that in translation into some languages (possibly even English) this thematization can be achieved only by a re-arrangement into the strictly chronological: *First X ... Then Y ... After that ... And next?* Certainly, the first translators of Milan Kundera's novel *The Joke* thought this kind of chronological sequence important enough to reshape the entire story (Kuhiwczak 1990:125).

Third, although the thematic dynamics of the text are of interest and not to be neglected, many translators may well have other priorities: what is *the Minamata disease?* should they provide an explanation for the target reader? and how will they deal with *avant-hier*, for which the translation is not so obvious? Most translation takes place in real time; priorities have to be set; and anxious calculations of theme-rheme may not be the most important.

Nonetheless, the breakdown of thematic structure can be important, as in the following sentence taken from a translation telling people how to handle 'Dangers Induced by Electric Current': *If nobody can remove the current, place on an insulated stool.* (By contrast, there are no thematic problems whatsoever in the sentence prior to this: *If the tension is over 1000V, remove the current and expect the fall of the victim if he is suspended.* The only problem here is calculating the speed of one's exit.) Thematic disruption is not just found in translation. The English newspaper *The Observer* in May 1994 quoted: *[Her] son was killed by a car going through a red traffic light. He was let off with a fine.*

Because thematic breakdown can lead to incoherence, thematic structure does require attention (no one would translate literally a very common

Russian structure such as *Funny, of course, the supposition ...*). And yet this is probably one area where seasoned translators in particular feel free to shift things around to their heart's content without regard to any theory. An analysis of translations of Gabriel García Márquez (Munday: research in progress) shows that the American translator quite happily moves adverbial phrases about without any sense that she might be disrupting a carefully planned pattern of theme-rheme information flow. This may mean one of three things: either the translator knows, consciously or unconsciously, that theme-rheme order is different in Spanish and English; or she doesn't know and doesn't care (unlikely given the quality of her work); or in many cases it doesn't really matter what comes where in the sentence as long as it's comprehensible. In which case, Nida was right to respond to Munday's research by invoking simple 'variability': a phrase that 'feels fine' in one position one day may simply 'feel better' in another position the next day. After a rapid survey of work done on the subject, Gallagher (1993:152) comes to the conclusion that "it is misleading to suggest ... that the theme-rheme organization of the source text must be preserved at all costs".

Indeed, unskilled translators may produce clumsy translations by unthinkingly reproducing source-language thematic structures. One offender here is the French clefted structure *c'est ... qui/que* .... Although French, like English, has quite strict word order, and is therefore forced, like English, to make use of this and other clefted devices to 'landscape' the information structure of sentences, the density of usage is not the same, and too many 'it is ... which' structures will be stylistically clumsy.

In summary, then, although the concepts of theme and rheme are useful to translators, more useful still is being able to interpret the reasons why things are put where they are in the sentence (focus, emphasis, contrast, presupposed knowledge, narrative presentation, sentence rhythm, etc.) and the various means for achieving those effects in the target language. Equally useful is the ability to decide whether or not, in a given translation situation, such things are worth attention.

For the sentence *In France, we do this search for our customers*, we earlier proposed an alternative translation. Both sentences used devices (*we, do, this, our, already*) which show that this sentence cannot be the first in the text. They can only be understood because they refer to information given earlier in the text. They are signals back to that information and they bind the present part of the text with its earlier parts. They give cohesion.

Cohesion

Properly maintained theme dynamics is just one of the ways a text is held together. Two other binding agents are cohesion, which is normally defined as the use of grammatical or structural devices to guarantee text integrity, and coherence, which is defined as the conceptual or semantic network that glues the parts of a text into the whole. You will not, of course, be surprised to be told that there are other definitions. Eggins (1994:87) defines coherence as the relation of the text to situation and genre, in other words as something external to the text, while cohesion is defined as a text-internal dimension.

By Eggins's account, if, in the middle of a sun-baked desert at high noon, I say *Turn on the light please*, I will be judged to be situationally incoherent. If, as the arresting officer at the scene of a crime, I replace the words *I shall now apprise you of your Miranda rights* by the words *Now, listen up you little piece of shit*, I shall be deemed generically incoherent. If I produce the French sentence *Il veux qu'elle est heureux*, I am being not incoherent but incohesive at a very basic internal level because the -*x* should be -*t*, the *est* should be *soit* and the *heureux* should be *heureuse*. Although a French person would make sense of my sentence, they would have to work harder to do so because I have demolished the basic grammar links that relate items to one another in a sentence and beyond.

Cohesion is one of the more interesting aspects of textuality, one that receives a great deal of attention in certain kinds of literary criticism but which is often all too easily overlooked in the translation situation.

There would seem to be two general ways of achieving cohesion, although it is difficult to define them in a way that avoids overlap. On the one hand, there is a set of clearly grammatical devices such as the sequence of tenses or junctives that organize the text in time, space and logic. On the other, there is a set of lexico-grammatical devices that are used for maintaining links of identity between items of semantic information in the text.

Cohesion through repetition

The most obvious device for holding parts of a text together is simple repetition, or 'recurrence', to use the technical term, as in *The group has been holding meetings... The meetings have been kept under wraps*. Too much repetition can be a bad thing, so a variation on recurrence is 'partial recurrence', which is to repeat the item in a different grammatical form, as in *I was moved by a feeling of ... Today I feel ...* (from a Russian text where the equivalent words were *chuvstom/chuvstvuiu*).

In the case of parallelism, a grammatical structure is repeated with different content, while paraphrase is the opposite: the same content in a different structure. A partial example of parallelism is the German *Tiefsinn, Unsinn, Scharfsinn*, which also demonstrates the greater effect of parallelism when it is supported by morphological structure rather than simple word class. The English translation of the German would be *profundity, non-sense, acuity*, which can rely only on the traditional rhetorical device of a ternary structure without any sound echo to bolster it. The same is true of the ternary but non-rhyming *simple, self-evident, monotonous*, translated from a Russian text in which, unlike the English, each word ends in the same sound. Clearly, deliberate repetition in a text may be a translation problem if it cannot be replicated.

Cohesion through ellipsis

Another way to hold text together is, paradoxically, by missing bits out, a device known as ellipsis. According to de Beaugrande and Dressler (1981:68) this phenomenon is not very well understood, since most linguistic research has concentrated on so-called 'well-formed sentences'. Consequently, although it should be a grammatical matter and of little importance for translation, coverage in grammar books tends to be very patchy.

Ellipsis can act in apparently bizarre ways. In English, for example, the subject of a sentence can be ellipted in the main clause but not in the subordinate clause: we can say *He's good at his job. Knows what he's doing*, but not *He's good at his job because knows what doing*.

From the point of view of translation it is important to know what each language is allowed to miss out and in what circumstances. Vinay and Darbelnet, followed by Vázquez-Ayora, seem to envisage three types of ellipsis in the translation situation.

First, there is the ellipsis that can only be resolved by reference to world knowledge or the situation. Such things as *SVP* or *Haut*, which are ellipted in the extreme, require cultural knowledge of how a specific society organizes public messages for economic communication: the first means *Keep off the Lawn* in Canada, while the second means *This Side Up* (Vinay and Darbelnet 1958:173). Knowing how to arrive at *Hello, stranger* from the French *On ne vous voit plus* (Vinay and Darbelnet 1958:175) requires knowledge of linguistic routines that are not always in the dictionary.

Second, there are cases of language-specific economy, which many source-language speakers will not regard as ellipsis. *We'll price ourselves out of the market* (Vinay and Darbelnet 1958:185) will not be considered elliptical by English speakers; it only becomes so in comparison with one of several likely French translations. Similarly, *He laughed his approval* (Vázquez-Ayora 1977:358) will be thought elliptical only in relation to the Spanish equivalent 'He approved it with a smile'. Nonetheless, such examples illustrate a widespread phenomenon in which the economy of an English structure of verb + adverbial usually needs to be diluted in translation, often by an inversion of the semantic content and grammatical structure: the adverbial phrase often indicates the end result of the action of the verb (*he cried himself to sleep*; *he drank himself to death*), and this has to become a less elliptical, inverted expression such as *he killed himself through excessive drinking*.

Three cases of ellipsis quoted by Vázquez-Ayora (1977:357) are matters of pure grammar, however: the omission of the relative pronoun and copula in *John thought Mary clever*, which may have to be restored in translation; the accusative+infinitive construction in *I asked them not to talk*, which must become *I asked them that they not talk* in many target languages; and so-called restrictives or concessives such as *Whatever his faults, he is a good friend*, where the elided elements often need to be restored in the target language (*Whatever his faults may be ...*).

A much more interesting type quoted by Vázquez-Ayora is problematic in two ways. It is the ellipsis of the kind *different levels of, and attitudes to, the communication process* (1977:356), although again whether this really is a case of ellipsis from the point of view of the source language is open to debate. The first way in which this kind of cohesion is a problem is that in many languages it would be considered an anacoluthon (a confusion of grammatical structures) to subject the same noun (*communication process*) to government by two different prepositions (*of, to*), and the structure must be replaced by an often lengthy periphrasis, going from economy to dilution.

The second way in which this is a problem is that in translating in the opposite direction, the movement from dilution to economy will often be lost. Faced with the Spanish phrase *que se ocupan de los diferentes niveles del proceso del comunicación así como de las actitudes que se han tomado frente a él*, the vast majority of translators will probably produce *which are concerned with the different levels of the communication process as well as the attitudes which people have adopted towards it*, perhaps because they will feel that the *así como* singles out the following phrase for treatment by co-ordination (*as well as ...*) rather than subordination (*levels of, and attitudes to, ...*). This is Levý's 'deceptive and treacherous' Category C equivalence, where the pressure of the source structure is so strong that even somebody translating into their native language will forget to use perfectly acceptable structures simply because they will never be encountered in the source, where they have no counterpart (Levý 1969:59).

The final category of ellipsis covered by Vinay and Darbelnet is at the borderline between ellipsis and our next topic, reference, because what is omitted in one language is represented (referred to) in another by so-called 'pro-forms'. The phenomenon of whether something is elided or represented constitutes the difference between languages that feel the need to provide the verb with all of its complementary bits and bobs, and other languages that are happy to wield the scissors. Thus, *We must tell him* is claimed to be short for *We must tell him about it,* and in some languages the *about it* must be expressed. The same is true of sentences like *He didn't say,* or comparatives like *He is cleverer than you think.*

Cohesion through reference

Languages try to avoid repetition by using shorter pro-forms to replace some longer item previously referred to. What these pro-forms are will depend on the language in question. In English they can be pro-nouns ('There was an old woman who lived in a shoe. *She* had so many children she didn't know what to do'), pro-verbs ('I know it, and so *do* you'), pro-complements ('Is this right? I think *so*'), and pro-modifiers ('He is a lazy, vicious, lying swine. *Such* people are best avoided').

Pro-forms are not the only way of achieving coreference in the textual chain. Repetition, partial repetition and synonymy serve the same purpose. A similar though not identical function is fulfilled by a class of words that have in the past been called shifters or pointers, but which are now usually called 'deictics' (from the Greek word meaning 'to point'). These include obvious pointing words like *this* and *that* (the demonstratives) or *here* and *there* (adverbs of place), and not so obvious pointers like *today* and *now* (adverbs of time).

In many cases deictics pose no problems for translators because there should be no reason to do any other than replace them with target-language equivalents. Deictics can, however, sometimes become a problem, especially in text types where the main purpose is not just to convey information. When Macbeth murmurs 'Tomorrow and tomorrow and tomorrow creeps on this petty pace', there should be no strictly referential need to replace the deictic by anything other than the target-language word for 'tomorrow', but aesthetic needs might dictate otherwise. (The comic writer Paul Jennings pointed out that Hamlet's anguished cry of *mother, mother* sounds like the bleating of a demented sheep when translated into French, while the scary *Hamlet, I am thy father's ghost* sounds distinctly unscary in Afrikaans: *Omlet, ek is de papa spook*).

Many translators, however, are familiar with the problem of deictics such as *recent* and *forthcoming* (*According to a recent report ...*; *In a forthcoming publication ...*). These will usually be out of date by the time a translation appears, and if it is the publisher's policy to avoid outdated references the translator could be faced with a not inconsiderable amount of research to replace the word *recent* with an actual date and to check whether *forthcoming* has finally come forth (translators should always insist on a separate research fee whenever appropriate; authors should stop using *recent* to give the impression of being bang up to date in their specialist field; *forthcoming* is unavoidable). A comparable translation problem posed by the deictics *we* and *you* will be dealt with briefly in the section on pragmatics.

Other forms of reference should cause fewer headaches, since the thing they refer to, the referent, will be recoverable from the context. This should allow the correct treatment of minor problems of appropriate grammatical categories of gender, number, etc.

In some cases, what is being referred to can be retrieved only from the cultural context, which may be universal or more parochial. This is homophoric reference. If I say *Look at the moon*, people will know where to look, even if the moon in question is a paper moon in a school theatrical production (Luke Skywalker, by contrast, would have needed more information). When the movie *Now, Voyager* closes on the immortal words *Don't let's ask for the moon; we have the stars*, we all understand. If it had ended with *Don't let's go to the boondocks; we have the Quantocks*, that would have been more parochial, since the shared knowledge pointed to by the use of *the* is much more culturally specific, accessible only to a limited number of people

From the point of view of translation, such instances are not actually interesting as examples of the linguistic category of reference. The questions they raise are better dealt with under the heading of presupposition, which we shall deal with in the section on pragmatics.

Even more localized are references to items in the immediate communicative situation: a weary parent says to a fractious child *Do put that down, Nigel, before you break it* and we would have to be there to know what the fragile *that* and *it* is. Most written texts, however, will create their own situational context: *The fractious child seized hold of the priceless Ming vase. His mother sighed: 'Do put that down ... '*, and items can then be referred to by anaphora, referring back to something that came earlier in the text, or cataphora, referring forward to something coming later. If you have difficulty distinguishing these words pronounce anaphora as 'enough already' (we've been here before) and cataphora as 'cut forward' (to the future).

This kind of reference may be a problem in a lengthy text because there may be long gaps between the reference and its referent, so a good memory is required, as happened in a text which made a cataphoric reference to something called *the ADAV* which was not resolved until very many pages later into *Allgemeine Deutsche Arbeiter Verein*, which could not have been guessed from the context of its first appearance.

One type of reference that may turn into a niggle for translators is reference to the text itself, as in *The examples discussed above* ... or *As we said earlier* ..., since many translation commissioners will insist on these being replaced by precise page numbers.

The most interesting problem with reference lies in possible differences of use between source and target, although again this is an understudied field. Some languages, such as Russian, do not have a word for *the* to refer to something we are presumed already to know about, so translation requires a different linguistic structure such as word order.

Both Spanish and French use the demonstrative deictic differently from English to constitute reference links (French people with near-native competence in English can often be detected only from slight misuse of the words *this* and *that*). As Vázquez-Ayora says, rather obscurely, "The anaphoric reference of the Spanish demonstrative is weak and leaves a gap. The transition must be more gradual ..." (1977:342). He gives the example of *I wonder about that* becoming *I wonder if that is true* in Spanish; while *A problem like that* becomes *A problem of that kind*, and *This section* becomes *The present section* (1977:280). Similarly, Vinay and Darbelnet (1958:112) list a whole set of examples in which the demonstrative as sole reference is not strong enough in French and must be supplemented in various ways.

Parataxis and hypotaxis

The second major way in which a text is held together is through joining parts of it together using a variety of conjunctions or devices that imitate conjunctions. The sentence *I've got a cold. I'm going to bed* uses what is called 'parataxis', simply putting the two sentences side-by-side with no obvious cohesive link. The text receiver has to provide the cause-effect connection through situational coherence. By contrast, *I'm going back to bed because I've got a cold* uses hypotaxis, placing one clause in subordination to the other and making the nature of the link clear through a cohesive device.

Now, some languages are claimed to be more hypotactic than others. Vázquez-Ayora tells us, "if compared with English, French boasts of being a linked language, Spanish is so to an even greater degree" (1977:111), and he quotes examples such as *Then he came out and Smith gave him ...* translated into Spanish as *When he came out, Smith gave him ....* If I take a French text at random, I find the following succession of hypotactic structures: *Est-il permis ... sans se faire accuser ... Est-il possible de ... pour tenter de ... avant qu'elles ..., le marché permettant de....* Turning to a similar type of article in an English newspaper of comparable quality I find the following succession of paratactic structures: *Charges typically eat up... They account for more than ... But charges could be cut ... Labour is promising ... A spokesman said ...*

The preference of certain languages for hypotaxis may pose the kind of problem Vinay and Darbelnet evoke regarding the translation of the paratactic writing of Ernest Hemingway, where, as they say (1958:229), the 'mental habits' of the translator will sooner or later kick in and begin to modify the style. This has also happened with the French translation of *Kes*, where the translator, almost certainly without realizing it, has replaced simple juxtaposition by participial subordination.

The actual ways in which languages achieve co-ordination and subordination of textual components are essentially a matter of grammar; they belong not so much in books on translation as in grammar books or books on text linguistics, as in de Beaugrande and Dressler's discussion of conjunction, disjunction, contrajunction and subordination (1981:71-74). Nevertheless, as part of their understanding of how a text is constructed and functions, translators should be able to recognize not just the specific functions of cause, reason, time etc., but also the more general functions of elaboration (restating or clarifying), extension (adding to or modifying) and enhancement (extending by specification) (Eggins 1994:105-106). They should also know (i) the extent to which their target language is hypotactic or paratactic in expressing these links in given text types; and (ii) whether, in particular, complicated subordination structures work in the target language.

The answer to (i) is still surprisingly impressionistic. Even though the concepts of coherence and cohesion, like that of theme and rheme, are now quite old, they still do not form part of the standard description of a language. All of the many books on the world's languages provide excellent thumbnail sketches of the phonetics, grammar, syntax and morphology of each language they cover, but nothing on how they handle texture, although there are isolated studies on the subject for specific languages.

The answer to (ii) depends of course on a variety of factors, of which the most important will be a trade-off between text type and information load. Take a sentence such as the following (translated from French):

The American president threatening to impose a steep tax on imports of white wine and the British press holding Jacques Delors up to public ridicule, are they using a similar ritual ...?

This literal translation is, of course, an anacoluthon. The first obvious solution is to form a correct English interrogative sentence (with careful use of commas to avoid ambiguity):

Are the American president, threatening to impose a steep tax on imports of white wine, and the British press, holding Jacques Delors up to public ridicule, using a similar ritual...?

The problem with this is that it requires readers to hold on to a lot of grammatical and semantic information before they finally get to the verb. This load is not intolerable for certain types of audience, so the translator has to decide whether to (i) impose it; (ii) lighten it by clear hypotactic signalling (*When the American president ..., and the British press ..., are they resorting to a similar ritual ...?*); (iii) resort to parataxis (*The American president ..., and the British press ... Perhaps they are trying to ....*

One area of translation in which the maintenance of cohesion suffers is in the translation of film, where the German researcher Herbst (1994:178-84) has found faulty use of the German equivalents of pro-forms, ellipsis and repetition. Given the specific constraints of this form of translation, it is doubtful whether the situation can be improved. But cohesion can also be impaired in written translation. Trainee translators in particular can produce nonsense without realizing it, and cohesive failure is often part of the problem.

Coherence

'Coherence' is the twin of 'cohesion', but it is a rather more difficult concept to define. It involves not only such matters as the conceptual logic of how a text is structured, which will often be reflected in cohesive devices, but also knowledge of such things as subject matter and how the world works. A good text producer will make sure there is a network of meaning relations both within the text and between the text and the real world to act as the Ariadne's thread for the reader.

One approach to coherence is found in scenes-and-frames linguistics, which, as we said earlier, has something in common with situationalism and contextualism as regulated patterns of behaviour. Definitions of scenes and frames vary from author to author. De Beaugrande and Dressler (1981:90) define a 'frame' as an internalized global pattern of knowledge about actions, objects and so on, so that we could, if asked, list the ingredients of a wedding ceremony or a graduation day. 'Scenes' (also called 'schemes') would be global patterns in which the knowledge is arranged in an appropriately structured form, so that in open heart surgery we know that we must anaesthetize the patient *before* we wield the scalpel.

Snell-Hornby (1988:82-6), who uses the definition of 'frame' as simply the linguistic form that triggers scenes, has attempted to show how the concepts might apply to translation in text analysis and production. Taking a newspaper article about the rescue of children from the ruins of a hospital in the aftermath of an earthquake, she finds three frames in the headline ('babies saved', 'Mexico', 'hospital ruins'), which are intended to activate two scenes ('there was an earthquake in Mexico', 'other babies have been found alive in the hospital ruins'). She then segments the body of the text into a series of scenes. By this point, however, she no longer seems to be using the word 'scene' in the sense defined above but quite simply in the sense of a scene in a play, since she merely gives each text segment a descriptive label such as 'police car with dogs', 'airport with rescue team', when you would expect 'airport' to be one scene-activating frame and 'rescue team' another. These scenes are then supposed to be "reconstructed into frames of the English language". In order to do this, she lists the scenes and indicates in note form what information is to go with each before finally producing a translation of the text.

This would appear to be a rather odd translation strategy: how many translators other than interpreters reduce the original to note form before doing a translation? Snell-Hornby's aim is to demonstrate her overall belief in a holistic approach to translation as opposed to a word-for-word approach, but the actual translation she produces differs from the original only in her decision to add explanatory information not in the German (the date of the earthquake and the hospital name, for example) and to replace the cultural reference *returned to the Bundesrepublik* by the hypernym *returned home*. There is nothing to indicate that a scenes-and-frame analysis has provided any more help with this translation than a good old-fashioned look at the context and the target readership. And the same is true of Kussmaul's explanation (1995:94-97) of why it is wrong to translate 'How many bedrooms?', which is a frame for activating the English scene 'house size', by the German 'Wieviele Schlafzimmer?', which activates the German scene 'sleeping and/or sex'.

In theory, since the translator produces a text on the basis of an already existing text, the coherence should be maintained if the translator knows enough about the subject matter to avoid wrong lexical choices. Even where cohesion is damaged in translation, as it often is, coherence of a kind may still be maintained. The translator who wrote *If, on the other hand, as big a partisan as Schmidt came to say last in Strasbourg, the blossoming of the European idea is only tenable as a US protégé* has produced a text that is a mess in terms of cohesion, but still sufficiently coherent. The same is true of the following extract from an advert for a cutting machine: *It is important for the user to dispose of a machine quere of the production capacity lies higher man his real needs. This provides a more supple action and an ever satisfaction giving production.*

Translation as text

So far we have been looking at how linguistic concepts assist in the production of translation at the textual level. But it is also possible to have a textual theory of translation, of which the last two examples are a good illustration. Educated native speakers writing directly in their native language are unlikely to produce the kind of mess we see in these two texts. So why does it happen in translation? Is it just the result of ignorance and inattention, or are translated texts systematically different from original texts in linguistically describable ways?

One of the first to analyze this phenomenon was, yet again, the Czech scholar Levý back in 1963 (although his work now seems to exist only in its 1969 German translation). His research highlighted two trends in translation. First, a process of lexical impoverishment takes place (Levý 1969: 110-11) because translators tend to choose more general and therefore more colourless vocabulary and because they reduce lexical variety by using fewer synonyms. Second (ibid:117), translators intellectualize the translated text by making it more logical, by explicitating the implicit, and by formally representing syntactic relations.

For a long time these phenomena were treated as translation mistakes under the pejorative heading of 'translationese', also called 'the third language' by Alan Duff (1981) who provides a detailed analysis of what produces translationese. Subsequently, however, research has concentrated on this phenomenon as a defining feature of translation as text and there has been an attempt to find universals of translation. The work of Blum-Kulka (1986) and Baker (1993), among others, has found evidence to support Levý's experiments, leading to the so-called 'explicitation hypothesis' which states that translations will as a general principle be more explicit than the original text.

Baker (1993:243-45) also suggests that translated texts will simplify and disambiguate, naturalize and normalize in relation to originals. Toury (1995:286-78) has brought the results together in his 'laws' of translation, one of which relates to the tolerance of specific languages for translationese, or 'interference'. This research, which is much facilitated by the use of computers, will continue to yield insights into how translations are their own kind of text.

9. Text Functions

Language functions

The devices used to build sentence perspective, cohesion and coherence are not selected at random. Out of the possibilities offered by language, we will choose those best suited to our aim in communicating. The text receiver will also attempt to link what we are saying to some kind of aim. This notion that all forms of behaviour can be described as serving a function is an old one. Some optimistic eighteenth-century philosophers believed that the behavioural function of the stripes on a melon was to guide the knives of human beings. The modern anthropologist will tell you, more plausibly, that your dog's face-licking behaviour is designed not to show affection but to make you regurgitate food. In a more tasteful vein, the Roman philosopher Cicero declared that language was also function-oriented behaviour and served three major functions: *ad docendum, ad delectandum, ad movendum* (to instruct, delight and move).

However, none of these functions seem to be involved if I murmur *Dreadful weather, isn't it* to an acquaintance in the street (although it is not inconceivable that I want to make him feel miserable). Consequently, later scholars have tried to set up more inclusive taxonomies of language functions that would incorporate just such linguistic behaviour as this. One of the most famous comes from one of the greatest of scholars to have worked in linguistics, Roman Jakobson, who related the function of an utterance to the element of language at the centre of attention. Different authors use different terms in this domain; the ones below are taken from Holmes (1992:286).

If an utterance is built on the following parameters:

Sender, Code, Message, Subject Matter, Channel and Receiver

then focusing attention on one of these yields the following language functions:

1. Sender: Expressive: using language to talk about oneself, as in *I feel pretty, oh so pretty*;
2. Code: Metalinguistic: using language to talk about language, as in *You say tomahto I say tomaydo*;
3. Message: Poetic: using the forms of language for aesthetic effect, as in *Bebop a lula a sham bam bam, tutti frutti* or *the murmur of doves in immemorial elms and buzzing of innumerable bees*;

4. Subject: Referential: using language to pass on information, as in *I just met a girl named Maria* or *We're all going on a summer holiday*;
5. Channel: Phatic: checking to see if the channel of communication is working or not, as in *Testing, testing, Mary had a little lamb, 1, 2, 3, testing*, or *Is there anybody there?, said the traveller, as he knocked at the moonlit door*;
6. Receiver: Directive: using language to get people to do something, as in *When you walk through a storm, hold your head up high and don't be afraid of the dark.*

We can safely assume that all these functions will be represented in all languages, although not necessarily to the same degree. In some cultures it is positively impolite to talk about oneself, while in others it is the height of Freudian repression not to. The directive function may be quite baldly expressed in some cultures, but wrapped around in politeness formulas in others. Indeed, within a given speech community the appropriate forms for a directive can vary enormously, from the straightforward imperative via the roundabout question to the opaque allusion, depending on the dimensions of register discussed earlier. The translator's job is to know not only the forms available but the correct circumstances in which they will be used.

The phatic function, in addition to actually testing the physical channel, also includes the means whereby a speaker simply maintains contact with someone. This can be either by the exchange of trivia or by the use of so-called contact parentheses such as *so you see* or *if you get my meaning*. It is to maintain phatic communion that a dentist will ask you some trivial question just after he's filled your mouth with sharp metal objects. Since this function is largely a spoken one, its importance in written translation will be in dealing with representations of speech. One obvious form of phatic communion in writing is the rhetorical question, which serves the purpose among other things of keeping the reader alert. However, as we have pointed out before, the use of the device varies between cultures. It would be quite unusual in English, but not in Russian, to have a stand-alone paragraph consisting of just one question, as in *What was the reason for this?* Russian can also, unlike English and other languages, use an exclamation such as *Hurrah!* on a line of its own (to express irony, I'm told).

Of the other language functions, obvious difficulties are posed for translation by the aesthetic function, too many to occupy us here. Rather less obvious may be the difficulties posed by the metalinguistic function, although they are closely related to the aesthetic function since they are often based on properties specific to the source language. Research in this area has been done by Zimmer (1981:127), who explains, for example, why a literal translation of the alliterative *horrible Harry* into French *horrible Henri* does not work, except on paper, because the *h* is silent in French, and so must be replaced by something like *affreux Alfred*. The only reason why this substitution is acceptable in its context is because it is taken from a book on linguistics, where the sole aim is to present information about the poetic function of alliteration. If Harry had been a name in a novel, then no such substitution would have been possible without running the risk of cultural adaptation.

This is the reason why some other metalinguistic translations quoted by Zimmer (1981:124-5) work only within limits. One of his examples is an incident taken from the nineteenth-century French novel *Le Rouge et le noir* in which the young hero betrays his humble origins by making a spelling mistake in the French language. The mistake he makes alters the pronunciation of the word involved, which allows his aristocratic employer not only to point out the mistake but also to repeat it mockingly in conversation two pages later. How this is handled in translation shows the decision-making process facing translators, how they also may not carry through completely the solution they opt for, and what sort of strain they put on the readership.

In the Finnish translation of *Le Rouge et le noir* the French word is retained, so that Finnish readers who can't pronounce French will not get the metalinguistic joke. In the German and Hungarian translations the French spelling mistake is transposed into a spelling mistake in the target languages. The Hungarian translation, however, is not followed through into both the microcontexts in which it is needed. The German translation is followed through, because, quite fortuitously, the offending word in French lends itself to literal translation with a misspelling that alters the pronunciation. However, although the limited local function is retained and made accessible to German readers, the larger aesthetic function is damaged because of the oddity of having French characters writing German.

An interesting micro-study by Nord (1995) shows the importance of this area of linguistics to translation by relating the language functions (to which she gives slightly different names) to book titles and newspaper headings in several European languages. She has found, for example, that three functions are essential and three functions are optional: a title *must* be distinctive, metatextual and phatic, but only *may* be referential, expressive and appellative (1995:266). In other words, a title must stand out, behave like a title, and make contact with the reader. A title may, but does not have to, tell us what the text is about, give the author's attitude to it, and provide an impulse for the reader to buy it.

In Nord's corpus of titles, the last three functions occurred in proportions of 100:30:6 respectively, although children's literature shows a higher incidence of the expressive function. Nord finds that German titles tend to be followed by a subtitle. The phatic function is achieved in all languages by having quite short titles which are easy to remember. And the referential function can be totally destroyed by a bad translation: *Die sündigen Engel* for *The Turn of the Screw* suggests pornography, while the literal Spanish translation is nonsensical. This brief account will serve to show the usefulness to the translator of knowing how language functions operate at a microtextual level. Yet texts also have functions at the macro level.

Text functions and types

Reiss and the monofunctional approach

The concept of text function has been the basis of various attempts to make translation 'scientific', or objectively justifiable. One of the pioneers in this work was the German scholar Katharina Reiss, who was keen to avoid a situation in which "the door is open to the caprice of the translator" (1971:31). Her work actually began as an attempt to find a better basis for judging the quality of a translation. Since not every element of the original can be preserved in translation, it makes no sense to judge a translated text in the traditional manner of picking out a few items to comment on. We should begin by determining the text type. For Reiss (1971:53), "If we have done this, then – since the text type co-determines the appropriate translation method – we can begin by investigating whether the translator has correctly followed the hierarchy of what must be preserved".

Since text type will decide our translation strategies, it clearly becomes important to have a system for deciding what type the text is. The distinction made by Cicero all those centuries ago was taken up by Reiss, via the German scholar Bühler, under the headings 'informative', 'expressive' and 'operative'. Bühler contended that all three functions figure simultaneously in any utterance. Reiss also accepts that there will be many "intersections and mixed forms" but believes that one function will predominate (1971:32).

Each language function will have a corresponding language dimension: logical for the informative, aesthetic for the expressive, dialogic for the operative type, and to each text function will correspond a global text type: the informative function will produce content-centred text types, the expressive function will give form-centred text types focusing on the sender, and the persuasive function will lead to behaviour-centred types focusing on the receiver. In the process of assigning a text to its type, we may have to let go of some traditional notions. Thus, an advert is not primarily informative so much as persuasive while 'trashy literature' of the bodice-ripper and airport variety is not expressive but informative (Reiss 1971:32-3). From this perspective, in other words, a text like *Probably the best lager in the world* is not a piece of information but an attempt to make you buy the beer, while *The steely blade flashed in the moonlight; a cry rang out across the lake; and Vlad the Vicious was no more* is not to be treated in the same way as *When to the sessions of sweet silent thought I summon up remembrance of things past* but in the same way as *The Japanese economy is due for a strong export and investment revival.*

The rather neat symmetry of Reiss's classification is disrupted by the need to include a further text type that is governed not by function but by extraneous factors such as medium. This is the audio-medial text type such as a radio play, a film or an opera, and it may intersect with any of the three others.

Each major text type contains subdivisions into numerous text sorts, such as lyric, play or novel for the expressive type, text book, report and essay for the informative type, and sermon, propaganda and advert for the operative or persuasive type. In her second book on the subject, Reiss arranges a selection of these text sorts into concentric circles (1976:19) to show how mixed forms emerge such as biography, which she says is a mixture of content-centred and form-centred text type.

It is, however, the overall text type, rather than the subdivisions, that will decide the type of equivalence to be sought and the translation strategy to be followed.

If the text function is to provide information, then content must be preserved at all costs, and any 'flourishes of style' can safely be sacrificed to that purpose, so that the translation method will be 'plain-prose'. A flaw in the argument here is that this 'ain't necessarily so', as we shall see in the section on presupposition with an example from a famous economics text book.

If the text function is to produce an aesthetic effect, then the translation must also have such an effect. This type of equivalence is to be achieved not by reproducing the informational content, nor even by reproducing the means which produced the effect in the source language, since both of these are likely (although not necessarily doomed) to fail. We must rather use analogous means, following what Reiss calls an 'author-adapted (identifying)' translation method, to produce the same, or at least a similar, effect. If I want to translate *Clang, clang, clang went the trolley*, there is little point looking up the word *clang* in my dictionary, as if the informational content of the word mattered, since in both Spanish and French it is translated as 'to emit a metallic sound', which has no aesthetic effect, while in Russian the

105

word *lyazg* may well, for all I know, have the same effect as *clang*, but is a noun rather than an interjection.

This is not a subject to be belaboured here, since the translation of literature involves far more than linguistics, but Reiss's scheme comes unstuck at the edges in this category. Whereas 'subject-adapted' and 'plain-prose' make sense as translation methods for the informative text, it is far less clear what is meant by describing 'autorgerecht' and 'identifizierend' as translation methods. We shall return to this point below.

Finally, if the text function is persuasive, then equivalence is achieved if the SL and TL texts have the same persuasive effect, and the translation method will be what Reiss calls 'parodistic/adaptive'. According to this theory, if I want to sell a product internationally, then I may have to adapt the name and the jingle to local conditions. *Drinka Pinta Milka Day* is unlikely to work in any other language, while marketing the ski resort of Bastad in English will require a certain sense of humour. There is, however, a fundamental question about whether or not this text type deserves separate treatment. This is another point we shall return to below.

In addition to deciding the general translation strategy, the text type will also and inevitably influence specific translation techniques, and much of Reiss's first book is devoted to showing how this works for each text type in relation to linguistic factors (semantics, grammar and style) and the non-linguistic factors of the speech situation (place, time, etc.), while her second book does the same for just the operative text type. Thus, when it comes to handling objects, customs and so forth which are specific to the source language culture, Reiss enumerates the possible techniques of borrowing, calque, footnote and explanation available to reproduce these in the target language, but relates them to text type. Footnotes, comments and even interpolated descriptions are quite natural in many of the sub-forms of the informative text type, but out of place in the persuasive type, where borrowing and calque are more appropriate, while explanation is best for the form-centred text type, since it allows the insertion of brief additional material which provides the information needed to understand the text without overly disrupting the expressive form (1971:79).

Reiss is also aware that the function of the text may be altered in translation, so that we get adaptation, paraphrase, summary, rough translation, student cribs, scholarly translations, interlinear versions, and so on. She similarly recognizes that a specifically targeted readership may also influence what happens in translation in terms of censorship, adaptation and rewriting. Although she sees the legitimacy of such approaches, for which she prefers the word 'transfer' rather than 'translation', they fall outside the scope of her aim, which is to provide criteria for judging the success of a translation as she understands that term.

Reiss's work has been subjected to criticism on all fronts by Koller (1979:199-205). He doubts the legitimacy of recognizing only three language functions, although the 'additional' ones that he offers, such as 'to convince', 'to entertain', 'to instruct', can all be subsumed under Reiss's three; he questions the attribution of text sorts to text types, and it is true that allocating clichéd popular novels to the domain of the content- rather than form-centred text type betrays a view of literary form which looks even more narrow now than when Koller himself called it narrow; he rightly criticizes her use of the term 'translation method' to mean a general instruction to the translator rather than a specific indication of how the instruction is to be put into practice; when Reiss does indicate a specific translation method (when she says, for example, that in content-centred texts linguistic form should obey the laws of the target language), Koller can see no logical connection between the general instruction and the method, and can even think of cases where the opposite method is needed.

Koller supports this last declaration by quoting (1979:242) a translator of content-centred texts (the late-capitalist training of non-manual workers in Sweden sounds as content-centred as you can get) who decided to stay as close as possible to the original in order to convey the flavour of Swedish officialese. Sadly, however, Koller does not give us an example of what this meant for the actual language used.

Nonetheless, this is, in fact, the most serious criticism of the Reissian approach. There is quite simply no necessary link between text function and translation strategy. Just because we have identified a text function, and just because that function is, in linguistic and possibly also logical terms, superordinate to the other aspects of the text, that does not mean that we are led inexorably to any logical or 'translation-scientific' imperative to take this function as the overriding parameter to which we subordinate our translation decisions. Giving primacy to the function may seem like a sensible thing to do; and it may seem like a desirable thing to do; it may even, if the author is still covered by copyright, seem like a legal thing to do; but it is still not a necessary thing to do.

A translator still might choose to behave like the linguistically alert hooligan on the London Underground who by judicious use of a penknife transformed the informative text above the door, *Obstructing the doors causes delays and can be dangerous*, into the anarcho-revolutionary operative text *Obstruct the doors, cause delays, and be dangerous*. If you object to this manipulation of function, then you should be reminded that there was a time when the overriding function of certain sacred texts was precisely that nobody should ever under any circumstance translate them. But some people did, and they were put to death for it. And now, because of their courage, other people do, and they are fairly well paid for it.

Another major problem with the Reissian taxonomy, which will carry us through into the next section, concerns the serious doubts as to whether the so-called operative text really exists independently of the informative and expressive text types. It is possible to imagine a text that conveys nothing but information ($e=mc^2$) and also texts which are purely expressive (*eenie, meenie, minie, mo*, or concrete poems that randomly mix 'empty' words like *ping* and *pong*). By contrast, a persuasive text which is something fundamentally different from a simple combination of information and form is more difficult to conceive.

In fact, it is already skating on thin ice to say that $e=mc^2$ conveys pure information, since, as Kade points out, even scientific texts aim to have an effect (1980:81). They might, for example, want to blind you with science, or kowtow to the prevalent conventions of writing science, or use a façade of science to promote a racist ideology. The ice is equally thin under the contention that a concrete poem like *ping ping pong ping pong pong* is a purely expressive text, since deconstructionists would probably point to the ingrained Western habit of seeing things in rigid binary terms while feminists might resent the harsh masculinity of the explosive consonants and the hard vowel *o*.

This is one of the most frequent criticisms of function-based translation taxonomies: they assume a monolith where really there is multifunctionality. Although the overall aim of a text is important, we still have to concentrate on the mosaic of subtextual functions. Indeed, under the influence of deconstruction it is the mosaic, the text as fragments, which becomes the centre of focus, but that is another story.

The multifunctional approach

One of the main proponents of the text as a multifunctional object was Halliday, whose work is summarized in Eggins and Bell from a purely linguistic point of view and in Hatim and Mason from a translation point of view. This approach also tries to make a connection between text function, the categories of systemic linguistics, and those of register analysis, and in the process produces quite abstract concepts that may seem a long way from how you and I actually experience a text.

Most texts convey ideas and talk about human experience. This gives them an ideational (or experiential) function. This would seem to relate to the register parameter of field or domain. For most translators, equipped as they are with the 'plan of action' that Kade (1980:40) assumes all text producers to have, dealing with this function would certainly require prior knowledge of the subject matter and a willingness to fill any knowledge gaps by appropriate and often demanding research. It might also require some version of Holz-Mänttäri's recommended process of using a variety of highlighting and linking devices (arrows, underlinings, circles, etc.) to bring out the techtonics or thematic structure of the text (1984:131-36), although again the divorce between the examples provided by translation theorists and the cases dealt with by practitioners is highlighted by the fact that her method can only work on short texts of the kind used in the translation class.

The linguists, however, would have us go further than this and analyze the ideational function into the semantic categories of transitivity that organize language into propositional meaning. These categories consist of Actor, Process, Goal, and Circumstance, each of which can be differentiated in various ways. Thus, if the Process is material (an action or an event), then we have an Actor and a Goal, as in *The Treaty of Rome gave Europe a long-term goal*, but if the Process is mental, then actor and goal are best called Senser and Phenomenon, as in *The nations of Europe hoped for peace*. Similarly, the Circumstances of propositional meaning can be subcategorized as Scope, Time, Manner, Place, and so on (Bell 1991:124-29). So an analysis at this level would involve the translator in identifying in each phase of the text what processes involve what actors and goals and in what circumstances. This may all seem a far cry from translation, but Hatim and Mason (1997:10) show how the modulation of choices in this domain can actually alter the way we perceive a fictional character.

Most texts also relate the text producer to the text receiver in some way, even if it is only by refusing a relation as in a coldly impersonal scientific text. This interpersonal function would seem to relate to the register parameter of tenor and will often be analyzed by the translator charting the use of such things as personal pronouns, rhetorical questions, connotationally marked words, shared knowledge, and so on. The linguist, however, would relate this to the grammatical categories of mood, which are every bit as abstract as those of transitivity. They organize language into sentences in which the functions of subject, predicate, complement, and adjunct are filled with noun phrases, verb phrases and adverbial phrases and structured into different sentence types such as declaratives and interrogatives which may be modalized for possibility and frequency or for obligation and inclination.

Although it may not be so easy to see the link between such an abstract concept as the varying configurations of subject, predicate, etc. and the interpersonal function of the text, a moment's reflection will reveal that a high use of declaratives would suggest an expert writing from a position of knowledge and power, while the use of questions (rhetorical in the case of written texts) indicates somebody seeking the solidarity of support. Similar support-seeking would be suggested by the use of modulated declaratives such as *The authors of the report wonder whether ...*, while the use of modals such as *usually* or *perhaps* might reflect a desire not to be seen as a dogmatic expert but as somebody prepared to be flexible. It has also been claimed (Eggins 1994:193-95) that clear distinctions can be made between men and women in choice of mood structures which define the interpersonal function and the tenor of a text: men, according to Eggins, "give information but demand goods and services", while "women demand information but give goods and services"; "women are conversationally 'supportive', while men just sit back and perform" (1994:194).

In addition to expressing ideas and relating author to receiver, texts are also organized as texts. This is the textual function and is described in terms of theme dynamics and relates to the register dimension of mode. We have already discussed these in detail above and need not come back to them here.

What we can do is to give a brief indication of how these functions can be distorted in translation. Faced with a French text on economic theory written in a very authoritative and forbidding style, a student translator made a deliberate decision to alter the register and the text functions because he was genuinely convinced that such a style was unacceptable in English.

The extract he translated was not the beginning of the text. He decided to indicate this by showing that the theme *economic models* was not new by adding in *such as these* (*the disadvantages of models such as these*). Unfortunately, because, in the register terms of Language User: Social Class, he was not fully in possession of a mature writing style (the so-called Educated Middle Class style), he went on to make the same move twice more in the second line of his text, and yet again in the sixth line, producing naive and obtrusive repetition of the phrase *such as these*. A similar lack of skill led him to alter the tenor from highly formal to colloquial by writing about *the industrial side of international trade* and also to make a mistake in thematic linkage by using the connecting conjunction *due to* when he meant *owing to*, as well as turning the appositional clause *..., the three powers being Germany, Japan and the US* into a full sentence in brackets with a full stop but no main verb. In terms of the ideational function, although superficially the text was an accurate rendering of the subject matter, he introduced explicit or implied Actors where there were none in the original (*a criticism levelled at, may lead one, it is agreed that, one might add* *that*). But the main change was in the mood system, producing a tenor that was far more consultative than the original and an interpersonal function that seemed far more anxious to take the audience with it than to provide instruction. This was done not only by the use of modal adjuncts such as *generally* or modal operators such as *might*, but also by the use of verbs that incorporate modality into their meaning such as *tend* (usuality), *suggests* (possibility).

As we have suggested in our discussion of Reiss, there is no objection in principle to making these changes. Baker (1992:211) quotes a Greek translation from English in which the incidence of repeated items is higher than in the original, and assumes, since Greek speakers have no objection to this, that the translation conforms to Greek discourse patterns. Similarly, in the French translation of Frank G. Slaughters's *Puritans in Paradise* (which has the much steamier title in French of *Love in The Bahamas*), the tenor has been altered in the first few paragraphs by the introduction of no fewer than three rhetorical questions where none exist in the original: *He felt none of the usual urge* becomes *Where was his usual impatience ...?*; *It was impossible to believe* becomes *How to believe ...?*; and *Footloose as he was* is translated as *Was he not free as the air ...?*

If changes such as these are deemed appropriate, then the student translator just quoted was not behaving inappropriately. What one might challenge is the judgement concerning what is and is not possible in the target language. The Greek translation alluded to by Baker may well have been just as acceptable without the lexical repetition, just as the French translation would certainly have caused no waves without the questions. What we are dealing with here are the intuitive judgements of professional translators whose intuition may or may not be good and about whose training as text producers we tend to know nothing.

Hatim and Mason, who discuss text functions and types under the headings of expository, argumentative and instructional, rather than in Reissian terminology, and who try to delineate typical ways in which they might be structured, come to the by now familiar conclusion that "relatively little is known about the differences in the ways text structures develop in different languages" (1990:173). Baker gives some indications on the subject, and Reiss and Vermeer refer to research tending to show that descriptive passages are less common in modern Hebrew and medieval European literature than they are in modern European literature (1984:28) and that novels begin differently in different cultures (1984:39). We can add to this that listing is a much more popular device in French newspaper writing than in English. We'll see an example later.

Function-altering translation

What we actually do in translation does not follow on automatically from the knowledge that different languages handle things differently. Just as a text can have a dominant function, so too can a translation. The function of the translation does not have to be the same as that of the original. Kade (1977:33) has said that there are two types of translation: equivalent translation, which retains the communicative function of the SL text, and heterovalent translation (content-reworking), where the text takes on a different function in the target language.

This idea that a translation may function differently from the original was already implicit in Nida and Taber, according to whom "Even the old question: Is this a correct translation? must be answered in terms of another question, namely: For whom?" (1969:1). Hönig and Kussmaul also declared that there were two basic types of translation, function retaining and function altering, and that both were equally legitimate (1982:40), an idea pursued in the so-called *Skopos* theory of Reiss and Vermeer (1984) and the action theory of Holz-Mänttäri (1984). Nord (1991:9) puts it bluntly: "The function of the target text is not arrived at automatically from an analysis of the source text, but is pragmatically defined by the purpose of the intercultural communication". Indeed, she goes even further: "Functional equivalence between source and target text is not the 'normal' skopos of a translation, but an exceptional case in which the factor 'change of functions' is assigned zero value" (1991:23).

In support of this Nord quotes the example of a newspaper article on drugs written for young people and containing slang and drug jargon. If this text is to be translated for a comparable audience, the interpersonal function implied by the language should be matched, but if the translation were aimed at an adult audience, the language would not be understood and the text would not be taken seriously (1991:53). Nord admits, however, that such texts, although popular with teachers of translation, rarely get translated in 'real life' because they are written for the occasion and rapidly become obsolescent (1991:64). If they are to be translated at all, they require a specific translation approach. To get at what this is, we shall take a short detour into the vexed question of literal versus free translation.

The (in)famous division between the literal and the free approach to translation, which dates back to the Romans, has not been popular among linguists (although theorists such as Antoine Berman, coming from other orientations, have been happy to develop it). Albrecht (1973:24) calls the terms "problematic but very popular" and tries to provide a linguistic basis for them by describing literal translation as '*Bedeutungsinvarianz*' and free translation as '*Bezeichnungsinvarianz*', which is the difference between sense and denotation, and so corresponds to sign-centred and content-centred translation respectively. Catford (1965:25) adds the third category of 'word-for-word' translation and suggests that the categories "partly correlate" with the linguistic rank (or level) chosen as the translation unit. This would mean that free translation has no set unit of translation, shifting up and down the linguistic scale, but tending to be at the higher levels, "sometimes between larger units than the sentence", while word-for-word translation, as the name suggests, takes the word or the morpheme as its translation unit, and literal translation bases itself on the word as unit, but may be obliged to shift up to group and clause level in order to be grammatical. This has an uncomfortable consequence, however: a translation such as *Il pleut à verse* for *It's raining cats and dogs* (1965:26) is called a free translation, where most people would want to call it functionally equivalent.

Overt and covert translation

On the whole, however, largely because of the problems posed by definitions such as Catford's, linguists have attempted to describe translation typologies without using the words 'literal' or 'free'. In 1977, House postulated a distinction between 'overt' and 'covert' translation. An overt translation "is one in which the TT addressees are quite 'overtly' not being directly addressed" (1977:189), so that such a translation is quite visibly a translation. This situation arises when the source text is clearly linked to its time, culture or language, and specifically targets its source language audience. With texts of this type, the function of the original cannot possibly be matched in translation, so a 'second level function' has to be matched instead (1977:191). This proves to be difficult because on the one hand the status of the source text or author means that the text "has to remain as intact as possible" but on the other hand such texts often contain material (like puns, dialects, etc.) which "frequently necessitates major changes" (1977:192). The problem, as House admits, is "often insoluble" (1977:193).

A covert translation is one which is not marked as a translation but could just as easily have been written originally in the target language. Texts which can be translated in this way are supracultural, supralinguistic and supratemporal. "In the case of covert TTs, it is thus both possible and desirable to keep the function of the ST equivalent in TT" (1977:194-95). If the overt approach to translation is difficult, then the covert approach is even more so since the translator has to take account of different cultural presuppositions in the TL context (1977:196).

113

This distinction is similar to that proposed by Nord between 'instrumental' and 'documentary' translation (Nord 1991:72-73), a distinction which, like House's, is based on whether or not the SL text specifically addressed itself to source-culture receivers. If it did not, then it is legitimate to produce an instrumental translation, one which can act independently in the target culture in one of three ways: (i) by replicating the function of the original, where that is possible, with all the linguistic and cultural changes that implies; (ii) finding other functions for the text, as in translating adult books for children; (iii) replicating the effect of the original, as in the translation of poetry. By contrast, in documentary translation (which covers word-for-word, literary, philological and exoticizing translations) the target reader is put into the role of 'observing' a communication between SL author and SL readers rather than being an integral part of the communication process.

Much the same distinction, but one which became far more famous, was put forward by Newmark as the distinction between 'communicative' and 'semantic' translation. The first translation type aims at equivalence of effect, while the second aims to reproduce the semantics and syntax of the source text as closely as possible (Newmark 1981:39). In the first type, we are able to participate fully in the communication event, while in the second we are called upon simply to observe. Thus, to take Newmark's simple example (1981:54), the communicative translation of *Frisch angestrichen* would be *Wet Paint*, whereas the semantic translation would be *Freshly painted*. Given the function of the phrase as a warning that needs to be understood promptly, the communicative translation would be the most appropriate in most cases, and there are certainly translation situations in which the phrase could well occur (in a novel, for example, or possibly in a set of instructions or a on a bilingual notice), while the semantic translation might be used in a linguistics book as examples of how different languages word public messages. Note that semantic does not mean literal: *angestrichen* in German can mean a few things other than painted, but semantic translation still takes account of context and pragmatics.

One final approach to text function and translation is the four-term taxonomy proposed by Neubert (1978:197-200). His criterion is the same as House's: the relationship of the text to the source language and culture. From this he deduces four situations, which, he claims, "give rise to highly definite consequences for translation" (1978:197).

In Type I both SL and TL texts have similar goals based on general needs: these are scientific and technical texts, and also adverts if the TL culture has them. Such texts have the highest degree of translatability.

Type II texts contain information specific to the needs of the SL readership: these are official pronouncements, instructions, local press, literature concerned with social, economic and political themes, and so on. This kind of text is untranslatable. This does not mean that they do not get translated, but that commonality of interests between SL and TL may be hard to locate, and that the translator must know why a text is being translated that was not intended for a TL audience.

Type III texts are literary texts, which, like Type II texts, are directed at the SL audience but which are also of potential interest to all human beings. They are translatable within significant limits because of their formal features.

Type IV texts are written with the intention of being translated because their function is to inform the foreign audience about events in the SL country. Even though these texts, like those in Type II, are closely imbricated with the sender culture, they will still be highly translatable but will require a good system of feedback between translator and customer.

It is not clear to what extent any of these taxonomies is ultimately very different from the distinction made by Nida between dynamic equivalence and formal correspondence. Perhaps the main difference is simply that Nida was more predisposed to emphasize dynamic equivalence while later authors have attempted to show the conditions in which both forms are appropriate. However, this apparent even-handedness is not completely successful and tends not to avoid a certain degree of religious reverence towards the 'original text'. Indeed, Gentzler (1993:72) finds this reverence behind much of what he sneeringly calls the 'scientific' approaches to translation theory. It appears in particular towards 'great literature', which most of these authors are adamant requires a literalist approach, mainly it would seem on moral grounds rather than linguistic ones. Nik Zaitun tells us of a translation of *Macbeth* into Malay in which the word *God* was replaced by *Allah* and the word *sword* was replaced by *kris*. The tone of her argument suggests approval until she suddenly announces that the play has been 'mistranslated' (1994:94).

Talking about originals and translations aimed at specific groups of people has already taken us into questions of sociolinguistics, while talking about the functions of a text, how language does things and how it relates the participants in the communication act, has taken us into pragmatics. The next two sections of this book will look more closely at various aspects of these disciplines as they relate to translation.

10. Sociolinguistics

When we looked at register analysis we already began to consider sociolinguistic questions about the relationship of language to the social roles that people play and the impact of status and power on the language people use. Social class, ethnic origin, gender, age, regional origin and professional status all cause variations in the language we use. These are matters of extreme importance since the social status of languages has frequently led to civil strife and bloodshed. The importance that we attach to language as identity poses considerable delicate problems for translators, and translation can be one element in the struggle to develop and defend languages threatened with disappearance.

Sociolinguistics can either provide us with a total theory of translation or provide linguistic insights that help us with specific aspects of translation. There are not now many who would feel obliged to follow Otto Kade, a linguist in the former East Germany, whose communist-inspired sociolinguistic approach led him to write things like: "Adopting the standpoint of the working classes, standing on the ground of Marxism-Leninism, is therefore also the best guarantee in language mediation for scientificity and fidelity to the original" and to declare that the socialist language mediator should be personally convinced of the Marxist-Leninist class viewpoint and have a Marxist-Leninist education (1980:38-39).

There are, however, quite a few who would still follow Kade in his declaration (1980:43-44) that Western bourgeois translators and translation theorists are guilty of occluding social matters: "bourgeois theorists try to explain the socially motivated processes in language mediation as purely linguistic phenomena". There is an increasing body of literature, of which the work of Lawrence Venuti is exemplary, devoted to demonstrating how translations are made in a variety of ways to seem 'transparent' to the Western English-speaking reader by suppressing or naturalizing the foreign. Of course, it is also possible to work in the opposite direction. Indeed, well before Venuti, the nineteenth-century German philosopher Schleiermacher proclaimed the value of foreignizing translations: readers should have "the feeling that they are in the presence of the foreign" (in Störig 1963:54); a language should have a special linguistic area for translations, and the latter "must be allowed many things which should not be seen elsewhere" (ibid: 70).

Already in the fifteenth century the German translator Niclas von Wyle, explaining why he had produced the difficult literal translation *you find some loving old men but none loved* rather than the more comprehensible *you find some old men who love women but you find no old men who are*

116

loved by women, propounded the theory that translations written for "high-born and well-educated princesses" and "illustrious princes" should be more difficult than those produced for the "simple common and uneducated man" (in Keller 1861:8). Louis Kelly (1979:70) explains medieval disputes over the translation of the New Testament as a matter of deciding the appropriate social style according to the degree of sophistication of the target audience. The *belles infidèles* translations of seventeenth and eighteenth-century France were also based on a form of sociolinguistics: the people for whom these translations were made belonged to a social class which (in theory, at least) ordered its life according to concepts of *honnêteté* (decency) and *bienséance* (decorum). Translations were supposed to conform to the same concepts.

We can see some of these latter sociolinguistic effects in the eighteenth-century translations by the French author Prévost of the English author Richardson. The lower classes are refused a voice by transforming their direct speech into indirect speech reported by the higher-class hero, or, when the lower orders do speak, transforming their local accent as represented by Richardson (*she has tacken the logins but for a fue nites*) into impeccable French (Stackelberg 1971:588). Similarly, Othello's straightforward, soldierly *Her father loved me* becomes, in the translation of de la Place, the highly sedate and mannered circumlocution *J'avais eu l'honneur de me faire estimer de son père* (Stackelberg 1971:590-91).

In this kind of translation the entire approach is determined by a social ethos of what is right and proper. For translators who do not seek the goal of cultural dominion, there is still a problem of how to give voice in translation to language varieties other than the prevalent 'correct speech'. Two of these voices are constituted by sociolect and dialect. There is some overlapping between these 'lects', but a dialect is normally defined as a way of speaking typical of a group of people living in a certain region, and sociolects characterize groupings by social class, status, profession, and so on. You can see the overlapping when you consider that in many countries dialects tend to be spoken mainly by the 'lower' classes of the region, while the middle classes living in the same geographical space adopt the national sociolect.

In many cultures slang is typically a sociolect used by specific groups of people. It may be job-related, as in the slang of thieves, a lot of which may never become known to the general public or becomes known only patchily, as in phrases like *to do a creep* for a specific kind of house burglary, or words like *a twoccer* for somebody who drives, usually recklessly, a car which has been '*t*aken *w*ithout [the] *o*wner's *c*onsent'. Such words tend to be known only to the criminals and the police. Some of them (like *twoccer*) get taken up by the newspapers if there is a spate of such crimes, and will then appear in the dictionary. Others may never appear in a dictionary and will be as big a nightmare for the translator as unfindable acronyms. Slang may also relate to a pastime such as train spotting or pop music. In some cases, certain types of slang may be used largely by younger people as an expression of group belonging or to express trendiness. In any event, it can create problems in translation.

There is, of course, the problem of actually identifying the slang. English people not in the know may once have been puzzled to see a night-club entrance marked 'UB40' (it was the entrance for people claiming *u*nem-ployment *b*enefit), and British judges are famous for asking questions that show their ignorance of the common parlance. Those who do not belong to the right age group are unlikely to understand the sentence *Don't be an anorak*. Once they have expunged the embarrassment of ignorance, they will sooner or later be exposed to the equal embarrassment of continuing to use them long after they have fallen out of fashion with the groups who introduced them.

Knowing the slang is only half the battle, however, because you then have to decide whether the target language has anything comparable. This might seem simple. We would expect most languages to have slang forms and we would expect to be able to substitute them for one another. However, the type of slang, the density of use and the purpose of use may not be the same from one culture to the next. In the late 1990s young French people returned to the use of back-slang, or 'verlan' (the French word for 'backwards' written backwards). For example, *femme* (woman) becomes *meuf*, or *laisse tomber* (let the matter drop, forget it) becomes *laisse béton* (which actually has the accidental meaning of 'leave concrete'). A lot of these expressions are not known to the parents of the children using them, and sometimes not even to slightly older younger people.

Now, although the type of slang we are talking about here does exist in English, its density of use is quite low. My slang dictionary gives the word *deache* as back-slang for *head* and *essaff* as back-slang for *face*. Yet in a lifetime of living in England I have never heard either. This type of slang would, in other words, be largely untranslatable into English by its homologue not because the type of slang does not exist but because it is far less frequent and less well-developed. For that reason it was not much used in the subtitles of the film *La Haine* which makes considerable use of verlan.

In such situations, other means must be found, as in a case quoted by Shveitser (1977:63) where the lack, in 1977 at least, of a Russian slang term for *pot* meaning 'marijuana' forced the translator to do two things: (i) to compensate by transferring the linguistic effect further down the chain of the sentence since no slang item could be found for that spot, and (ii) to replace drug slang by criminal jargon by turning the stylistically neutral verb 'caught' ('if they're caught using pot') into *zastukat* meaning 'to denounce somebody to the KGB'. In Russian newspapers, cant, the slang of thieves, is often used in inverted commas to express sarcasm. This would not be the effect in other languages.

In addition to types of slang being unavailable, or used to different extents, the actual purpose or the effect of slang can be different between languages. In Claude Lelouch's 1976 film *Si c'était à refaire*, translated as *Second Chance*, the American translators of the dubbed version have a teenage boy saying things like *I'm top man on a totem pole and King Kong all in one*, *The other chick's kinda old but a sweetheart all the same. She gamme a pair o' wheels*, and *Hey, how high can a man get!*, which is young hip, whereas the original French would have been the kind of slang used by most generations of French people and therefore marked simply as informal. The German version of the film (*Ein Hauch von Zärtlichkeit*) goes in the opposite direction, saying only *I'm the pasha of Saint-Valéry sur Somme; she's really old but nice; she got me a bike; nobody ever died of envy.*

Slang seems to be quite regularly expunged or weakened in the translation of films. This was the finding of Hesse-Quack (1969:114) who quotes words like *moins emmerdeuses* translated as *nicht so kapriziös*. My own research has shown things like *Oh putain* translated as *No kidding* in the hit film *Les Visiteurs* (1993), while in *La Fracture du myocarde* (1990) (*Cross My Heart*), which is full of the kind of foul-mouthed slang so common among French children, the translators have not opted to find the functional vulgar equivalents so common among young English children: *Ça sert à rien de se faire chier* becomes *Why worry?*, and *T'es chiante comme une nana* is translated as *You're such a pain*. Note that where slang is toned down, it is not necessarily an act of censorship. As Hesse-Quack (1969:127) says, the target language might quite simply not have the range and strength of vocabulary to replace it, which lends support to the hypotheses of Levý and Toury in relation to the levelling and generalising tendencies of translation.

The opposite tendency can also be found, however. In the film *Stalingrad* (1993) neutral language is replaced by American slang: *Tatsächlich* is translated as *No shit*, while *Drecksack* becomes *Asshole*.

Other forms of sociolect can also cause problems for much the same reasons. The comic writer Afferbeck Lauder gave a lot of people some harmless pleasure during the 1960s with a little book called *Fraffly Well Spoken*, which contained short dialogues spelt in such a way as to imitate the pronunciation of the English upper middle classes, the so-called 'public school' pronunciation. *The sitweshns frott with dencher* is how they would pronounce *The situation is fraught with danger*. Translating such sociolinguistic levels into languages that are supposedly classless (as is claimed for both American and German) is obviously going to be difficult. In any event, as was the case with slang, we are unlikely to find one-to-one correspondences. As Shveitser says (1977:61), literature often uses social or regional variability as a means of characterization, but he believes it is often and inevitably levelled out.

One form of levelling found in film dubbing is to make thoroughgoing use of the American sociolect, for economic reasons. François Truffaut's *La Nuit américaine* (1973) (*Day for Night*) and Claude Lelouch's *Si c'était à refaire* are available only in American. This process can lead to quite bizarre consequences. The German children's film *Runaway Express* (1992) has been dubbed into an American which does not always sound quite right. The end credits reveal that the film had been dubbed by a company located in Wales, presumably using British actors instructed to use an American accent!

The problem, as we have seen in the case of *Second Chance*, is that this linguistic domination can also lead to unwarranted cultural transfer. In the same film, a French teacher speaking to his students is given the words *Hey, wow, man! You're all meatheads in this class!* which is not how French teachers speak to their students and does not match the speaker's sardonic facial expression (the German version has the more restrained: *Eine brillante Klasse habe ich da*).

Perverse though this example may be, it does suggest that Shveitser's rather pessimistic view that sociodialects are inevitably lost in translation is not always borne out by reality. There are more or less successful ploys for dealing with the problem.

One not very successful attempt is found in the French-Canadian film *Being at Home with Claude* (1992), where the subtitlers attempted to represent the nonstandard urban variety of Canadian French, known as 'joual', by what seemed like American gangster-speak: *What are you doing?* becomes *Whaddaya doin'?* This does not work, however, because it goes against the industry practice of making subtitles transparent and instantly comprehensible. The need to reproduce the accent mentally strains the viewer's language processing capacities in the already difficult subtitling situation.

Shveitser (1977:62) refers to another unsuccessful attempt to translate sociolect when he quotes a critic as saying that in the Russian translation of *Vanity Fair* "the English Joneses and Johnsons spoke the dialect of Moscow corn merchants". By contrast, Zimmer (1981:146) finds the German attempt to translate the Cockney lect of *Pygmalion* (later to become *My Fair Lady*) quite successful. However, the effect is not achieved by matching at the same linguistic level. The Cockney dialect is represented in the English text mainly by pronunciation and poor grammar, whereas the German translator uses not only indications of nonstandard pronunciation and grammar but also 'vulgar' lexis and syntax.

Something similar happens in the French version of the English novel *Kes*. The northern English dialect used in the dialogue passages should in theory be translated differently from the non-dialectal language of the narrative, but this becomes a problem for the reasons we saw in the discussion of register. Because there is no French dialect that is comparable to English Yorkshire, the latter is replaced by a sociolect. For example, the phrase *What's up wi'thee, shit t'bed?* represents dialect by pronunciation and vocabulary: the dialectal pronoun *thee* for *you*, the characteristic omission of certain sounds such as the loss of the *-th* on *with* and the reduction of *the* to *t*, usually pronounced as a glottal stop. The French translation *Quoi donc qu'il t'arrive? T'as chié au lit?* is not dialect but sociolect, using deviant grammar typical of the 'incorrect' spoken language of the less well educated, a translation move which may well be thought politically incorrect but which sadly matches popular perceptions. In *The Observer* of 15 December 1996 a recruitment consultant from the south of England is quoted as saying: "Let's face it – people with Scouse [Liverpool] accents sound whiny, and people with Brummie [Birmingham] accents sound stupid", while another says: "Generally, you are perceived to have a higher intelligence if you speak 'received English' [BBC English]".

Occasionally the translator may try to find an even more radical solution to dialect translation. Shveitser (1977:62) quotes the translation of the Doric Greek dialect in a classical Greek comedy into Nigerian pidgin, giving language like *Wusa ah go find una chiefs or wetin una de call dem leaders? Ah bring important news for dem.* It is also possible to find the Bible translated into rap language and other dialects. This kind of translation has such repercussions (literary, as well as religious, texts are sacred to many people) that references to it can be found in the strangest of places: one episode of the American TV sitcom *The Byrds of Paradise* discussed the advisability of allowing some schoolchildren to perform Shakespeare in Hawaian Pidgin!

Mishandling sociolects and dialects in translation can lead to laughable results. The translator Gregory Rabassa (1984:39) thinks that "The most appalling errors of translation are not the slips brought on by a misread word, but things like 'gosh darn' in the mouth of a drover". Rabassa, in fact, believes that "The transfer of local or regional idioms into another language ... must be listed as another of the impossibilities of translation" (1984:24). But the results of inept handling of sociolect and dialect can be far worse than laughable: they can lead to offensive stereotyping and to whole groups of people being gratuitously insulted. Hesse-Quack (1969:230), for example, found that German dubbing made an unpleasantly consistent use of the Berlin urban dialect to characterize socially inferior characters in foreign films.

There is also the problem of naturalizing dialects and their speakers out of existence in translation. Annick Chapdelaine (1994:12-13) has attempted to go against this trend by translating the Southern American dialect in a Faulkner novel into rural Québecois. She claims to be "motivated not by the desire to naturalize Faulkner, but to make him accessible to French-speaking people via Québec". But there has to be some doubt as to what is achieved by this. Writing something like *J'cré ben que je vas commencer demain* ('I think I'll start tomorrow) (Chapdelaine 1994:23) will certainly give a voice to the linguistic Other, but will not of course evoke the Deep South so much as the vastly different environment of rural Québec.

It is not at all obvious either here or in the case of *Kes* how an audience can find its way back from the local resonances of the translation to those of the original. Although this form of translation, somewhat confusingly called transparent to differentiate it from the kind of translation which renders the foreign invisible, has the noblest of aims, we should not delude ourselves as to what it can achieve. It takes us to the point where translation becomes impossible.

11. Pragmatics

An area of modern linguistics of considerable importance for translation, and on which great hopes have sometimes been placed, is pragmatics. This has been defined in a number of ways. If, following Neubert (1978:185-89), we define *grammatical* meaning as the relation between linguistic forms, and *semantic* meaning as the relation between forms and reality, then *pragmatic* meaning can be seen as the relation between linguistic forms and the participants in the communicative act. This definition, however, is broad enough to include sociolinguistics. So we might more usefully say that pragmatics studies how grammar and semantics are put together in order to *do* something with language. Pragmatics covers quite a number of things, including deixis, which we have already referred to. Here we shall pick out just three aspects that have attracted attention: presupposition, speech acts, and Gricean implicatures.

Presupposition

Presupposition can be a highly technical subject involving subtle logical distinctions. Experts in these matters seem dreadfully keen to know what kind of person would say *The King of France is bald* when there is no such person. Furthermore, as Hickey says (1993:89), "virtually everything written about presupposition is challenged or contradicted by some authority on the subject." Clearly these are deep waters, so let's keep our feet on the ground.

If I ask *Have you got any children?*, I am presupposing there is someone there to answer and that they understand English. I am further presupposing rather less obvious things such as the *ability* of the other person to respond (I'm not likely to ask the question of someone who is lying face down at the bottom of a swimming pool), and the *willingness* of the person to respond (I'm not likely to ask it of somebody who has just been fitted with a pair of concrete shoes and has other things on their mind). I am also presupposing their willingness or predisposition to answer questions of a personal nature.

I can derive the first and second of these presuppositions from the language used: the word *you* implies the existence of an addressee (which might be oneself) and the sentence is in English. It might also be possible to derive at least some elements of the other presuppositions from the language used since my utterance takes the form of a question, which presupposes answers. Let's use the completely untechnical term of 'linguistic presupposition' for these.

However, at least some elements of these presuppositions will be related not to the linguistic items in my question but to context, and beyond that to knowledge and culture: I am unlikely to ask the question if I am in possession of information that would make it unwise or unwelcome. I won't, for example, ask the question of somebody who is putting flowers on a grave marked *In loving memory of X, the only child of ...*, and I won't, in general, ask questions of a personal nature if I know my interlocutor comes from a culture of personal discretion, as in Japan, where they practise 'enryo', an attitude of personal reserve in social relationships (Simeoni 1993:176). There are, of course, people who will do both of these things, either because they are insensitive, offensive or cruel or because they get paid to do it (satirists). Let's call these 'nonlinguistic presuppositions'.

If I take my question one stage further and ask 'How often do you take your children to the zoo?', I am making yet more presuppositions, most notably that the person *has* children (the word *your* is the give-away) and that the person is in the *habit* of taking his or her children places (the words *how often* let this particular cat out of the bag). Again I am making other presuppositions of a personal and cultural nature. I am probably assuming that taking children to public places is a thing that people do, and I am assuming that zoos are a fit place for impressionable young people.

In fact, when you start taking a sentence apart to find out just what presuppositions it contains, you will find there are lots of triggers, both linguistic and nonlinguistic (contextual and cultural), that show that when we talk or write we make a very large number of presuppositions.

One reason for making the rather crude distinction between linguistic and nonlinguistic presuppositions is to make the point that the latter are of most interest to translators. If I have to translate a sentence like *The boy's done it again*, the presupposition that the boy has done it *before* should come out in the translation as clearly as it does in the original. The same holds true for other linguistic triggers of presupposition. By contrast, I can make no sense whatsoever of the sentence *We need Mohács*, because I do not share the cultural knowledge presupposed by the author. This is why the English translator produced the hypernymic translation *We need defeat* instead (Radó 1979:191), even though there is considerable loss in the translation.

Similarly, a literal translation of *A force de voir des Budapest sur nos écrans de télévision* can safely carry the presuppositions about television ownership and viewing habits, but will overlook the fact that few readers are likely to know what *Budapest* symbolizes in this case. Similarly, the student who produced the translation *He 'dies without a sound' like Alfred de Vigny's wolf* was wrongly presupposing a fair amount of cultural knowledge on the part of the reader: who was Alfred de Vigny and what exactly was his relationship with wolves (not to mention the question of why and how the wolf died and why part of the sentence is in quotation marks)? Such pragmatic problems assume increased acuity when the text to be translated includes deictic references to *we, us* and *you*, signalling an involvement that the target reader will probably not have or feel and leaving the translator to decide whether to retain the pronouns or replace them by appropriate phrases which will alter the tenor of the text.

Very few texts will be unaffected by presupposition. The problem is perhaps best handled by the concept put forward in German translation theory by Reiss and Vermeer and taken up by Nord of a text as an 'Informationsangebot', an offer of information, although people like Newmark (1996:91) dislike the ideology of translation as trade. The point of presupposition is that you save time by not supplying information for which there is no demand, since you believe it to be shared (unless there is a specific purpose to supplying it, as in *As a priest, you ought to know better than to use bad language*, where the person addressed presumably knows he's a priest but needs reminding of what goes with that). Most Hungarians don't have to be told that Mohács was the site of a military defeat, just as most French people don't have to be told what went wrong at Alésia. A writer in those languages can call up powerful complexes of knowledge and feeling very economically. Transfer these to another culture, however, and the presupposed information may not be there.

First, the translator may not share the presupposed knowledge, and if Durieux (1990:671) is right when she says that "the translator must, in any event, possess the knowledge that the author presupposes their readers to have", they must undertake research to acquire it, although in reality a lot of translation is done without it.

Second, the translator must estimate to what extent the target audience is likely to share the presuppositions. This is a difficult judgement to make and involves a delicate balancing act. Either the translator patronizes the target audience by treating them as if they know nothing and lack the means to find out, or the translator leaves them in the dark by not supplying what is needed to make sense of the text.

If the target audience is assumed not to know what is being talked about, the translator must decide what is the best way to pass on the information with a minimum of disruption.

As a trivial example, take the word *April* as a homophoric reference that may pose problems if you have to translate the words of the popular song *Though April showers may come your way, They bring the flowers That bloom in May* for a culture where April presupposes anything but rain. In cases like this, translator decisions will be governed by the function of the translation in the target culture.

As a non-trivial example take the case of the translation of an Inuit legend (Ireland 1989) in which the translator decided *not* to pass on cultural information, rendering a word meaning 'skins from seals less than a year old' as simply *sealskins* because the idea that the Inuit might kill and take the skins of baby seals would put them in a bad light with a Western audience enamoured, thanks to *Flipper* and *Free Willy*, with wide-eyed marine life. In other words, the translator needs to know not just what presuppositional information may be *lacking* in the target culture but what presuppositions *exist* in that culture which may 'proactively' influence the translation.

Even when translators have identified possible problems of a pragmatic nature, they may still get the translation wrong; or they may decide there is no problem but go ahead and make changes anyway. Thus, the famous economics textbook by Samuelson uses the image of a tennis ball and a wad of gum to make a point about economics: *Like a tennis ball (and unlike a wad of gum), [economic growth] is likely to bounce back from the full-employment ceiling into a recession* (1970:246-47). Presumably judging that *wad of gum* was less obviously comprehensible (or perhaps cultural imperialism) to nations less addicted to the substance, both the French and German translators decided to replace it, but they both got it wrong: neither the French object ('ball of wool') (1972:373) nor the German object ('medicine ball') (1973:328) display quite the same habit of sticking to the ceiling as does a wad of chewing gum.

In the same section the translators had to deal with the cultural reference to *policy makers in Washington*. The German version assumed, no doubt rightly, that *die Wirtschaftspolitiker in Washington* would pose no problems of presupposed information, although one might wonder about the effect of the 'foreign' allusion on a different audience. The French translator presumably also realized there would be no real problem with a literal translation but decided to make a stand against imperialism by replacing *Washington* with a specifically French allusion to 'the hero in René Clair's film *C'est arrivé demain*' (1972:374), which is about a man who can predict the future, something the policy makers would like to be able to do.

Speech acts

A second area of pragmatics that is claimed to be important for translation is 'speech act theory', which, like presupposition, is a matter of some controversy and dispute in linguistics.

The idea behind this theory, which originated with the English philosopher Austin, is that sentences do not just impart information but also perform an act. More precisely, they perform three acts: (i) the locutionary act is the act of making a meaningful sentence, so that the locutionary meaning of a sentence such as *Can you stop singing, Bruce?* consists of a question about whether or not a man named Bruce has the ability to quit the musical mode; (ii) the illocutionary act is what the sentence is intended to achieve, the use to which it is put; we'll come back to this in a second; (iii) the perlocutionary act consists of the effect of the utterance on the speaker.

Now let's go back to (ii). *Can you stop singing, Bruce?* might actually be performing one of at least two speech acts. One can imagine that our friend Bruce is stricken with a rare and mysterious disease called meloditis and has gone to see a doctor, who wants to know whether the patient can actually exercise any control at all over his vocal chords. Or, far more plausibly, one can imagine a situation in which somebody is highly irritated by Bruce's singing and just wants him to shut up. In the first instance, the illocutionary force would be that of a question, while in the second instance, in spite of the interrogative grammatical structure, it would actually be a command. In other words, the act being performed by a particular sentence is not necessarily given by its form alone but requires contextual information, and a corollary of this is that the same speech act can be performed in many different ways. As Sadock and Zwicky say (1985:191), "It is possible to use nearly any sentence type with the effect of nearly any other".

As for the perlocutionary act, in the first scenario the effect will be to elicit a response, albeit sung rather than spoken, while in the second case the perlocutionary force would depend on Bruce's personality and power status: he might shut up or he might sing more loudly.

In theory, a speech act involves all three of these elements, but in practice linguistic discussion has focused largely on the illocutionary act. The locutionary act is more a matter of pure semantics, while the perlocutionary act probably falls largely outside linguistics.

The concept of speech acts arose out of the notion that some sentences actually do perform an act, are indeed the *only* means of performing the act. For this reason they are called performatives. The obvious examples are *I name this ship the Flying Dutchman, I now pronounce you man and wife, I sentence you to be hanged by the neck until dead, You're fired* (although in theory the last example is not a performative because it does not begin with 'I'). All of these sentences can also be used in circumstances in which they are not performatives, typically in reported speech, as in *So what did you say next, Judge Jeffries? — I told the little swine I sentence ....* In theory, therefore, such speech acts require 'felicity conditions' to make them into performatives and to make them work, in the same way that locutionary meaning requires truth conditions. I cannot truthfully say the king of France is bald if he has a full head of hair (or doesn't exist), and I cannot felicitously say *I now pronounce you man and wife* unless I am properly authorized to do so. Of course, in the real world neither sort of condition *has* to be satisfied: the world is full of liars and frauds.

Having delimited the obvious performatives, the question then arose as to what other speech acts might be fulfilled by utterances, and this is where the problem begins. Leech (1981:322) lists "statements, questions, promises, warnings, apologies, etc.", where the 'etc.' implies a possibly endless list, which would become unmanageable and therefore useless. There is also the question of whether, in cases where there is no explicit performative verb, we should postulate that one exists in the deep structure, so that a series of statements is a really a succession of declaratives with the words *I declare* left out.

We need not pursue these theoretical questions here, but rather turn to the matter of how useful it is for translators to know about speech acts. Hatim and Mason, for example, analyze a passage of English on the assumption that a translation will be influenced by the speech acts underlining the actual words used: "the translator will seek to relay the illocutionary force of each speech act in turn" (1990:61). In other words, in order to translate one of their examples – *I have compiled a bibliography ..., which I should be happy to send ...* – the translator should know that the speech act in the first half is a representative (seeking to represent a state of affairs), while the second half is a commissive (committing the speaker to a course of action). In reality, however, a fairly literal translation will in very many cases produce the desired effect without the need for the translator to know anything other than how to say *have compiled* and *would be happy to* in their target language.

Obviously, when a translator has to translate the more obvious ritualistic performatives (of the 'I now pronounce you man and wife' variety), then a literal translation will not do, and the appropriate form of words needs to be used. It is quite surprising, therefore, not to find these formulas in bilingual dictionaries. Other speech acts of the non-ritualistic kind, such as promising, betting and so on, should also pose no problem, since, as Palmer says (1981:166), "speech acts are probably independent of the actual language" (although he adds an immediate, second qualifier in the form of "at least to some degree"). Searle also accepts that "translations of the sentences in question will often, though by no means always, produce sentences with the same indirect illocutionary act potential of the English examples" (1975:68), just as Hönig and Kussmaul say of a sentence to be translated into German "However it is translated, the illocutionary force of the sentence would not change" (1982:80).

What may be the case is that different cultures use the same speech acts to different degrees, although the research done in this area is, like that on presupposition, disputed by the scholars. This may be especially true of so-called indirection, in which we avoid issuing a direct command by using *Can you ... pretty please?*, *Would you mind dreadfully ...?*, *Could I possibly ask you to ...?*. It will also be true of the speech act of cursing, but few of us have the thrill of translating those. In these cases of indirect speech act, "the standard forms from one language to the next will not always maintain their indirect speech act potential when translated from one language to another" (Searle 1975:76), so the translator will have what should be the relatively simple task of learning which forms work and which do not. As Searle says (1975:76), a literal translation into Czech of *Can you hand me that book?* "will sound very odd if uttered as a request", just as a literal translation into German of *Why don't you shut the window?* would not be taken to have the illocutionary force of a request (Hönig and Kussmaul 1982:77). Snell-Hornby has done a micro-study of speech acts in public notices in German and English and finds that although both languages have the same speech acts, there are differences in whether or not the addressee is specified and in the grammatical and lexical means used: English prefers imperatives and modal verbs while German uses nouns and past participles (1988:86-93).

Consequently, although it is true that in many cases speech acts will be preserved in translation without the need to identify them first, this should not be taken to mean that they pose no problems at all for the translator. Starting the translation of a philosophical text on cannibalism with the words *Not so very long ago* (the SL text began *When recently*) is to make the wrong speech act, turning an illustrative statement into a fairy tale. Translating a sentence which reads *These models concentrate on ...* into *These models tend to concentrate on ...* is to turn a statement into a judgement. Leuven-Zwart (1990:83) points to the effects of a simple switch between the speech act of questioning and the speech act of stating when *'Isn't life ...?', she stammered* is translated as *Pero eso no es la vida*, which transforms the character from feeling "perplexity and confusion" to being "cool and distant".

Even here, however, the judgement is not necessarily so simple. We earlier mentioned a French translation in which statements had been turned into rhetorical questions because the device is more frequent in French and is one of the ways in which French narrative achieves immediacy. So, although Leuven-Zwart is right in the case she discusses, such speech-act changes may be made for reasons of usage and be perfectly justified. What gives them their justification is that the translator is adjusting the text to the knowledge and expectations of the target audience. The translator is being polite. It is, of course, possible to be an 'impolite' translator, and that would have implications for the reader. There would be implicatures.

Implicature

The concept of implicature, originated by Grice, is based on the assumption that conversation is guided by a co-operative principle based on maxims of the kind children have drummed into them by parents and teachers: be polite, don't waffle, speak when you're spoken to, and so on. These maxims are, of course, frequently ignored or violated, as in the classic *Can you tell me the time? – Yes.* When that happens we don't necessarily assume a breakdown in conversation, but rather that something is being implied which the listener has to work out. If young Romeo is on the phone exchanging sweet talk with Juliet and suddenly raises the tone of his voice and says *Yes, OK, Bob, we'll work on the car tonight – after we've done our homework, of course*, Juliet at the other end of the line will probably ask *Has somebody just come into the room?*, rather than assuming a sudden and swift descent into lunacy on Romeo's part.

Grice himself postulated (1975) four maxims: quantity, quality, relation, and manner. The first means that you should give just as much information as is required (don't waffle, don't be curt, don't be mute). The second means that you should say only what you believe to be true (don't tell porkies). The third means that what you say should be relevant (get to the point, don't go off at a tangent). The fourth means that you should be clear. Other researchers have added to these a maxim of politeness, which says simply: be polite.

Although the concept, like many ideas in linguistics, was developed primarily for the analysis of spoken language, its relevance to the written language and therefore to translation is also clear. It could work both as a general theory of the act of translation – Holz-Mänttäri (1984) describes translation as 'intercultural cooperation' – and as an instruction to translators to learn how the maxims are applied in the languages they work between and to act accordingly.

The politeness principle could be used in invoking the non-translation of offensive material into cultures where it is not customary to cause offence in writing, although this means violating the quality principle, since the translator will not be giving an accurate and truthful account of the original. The principle of quantity of information has clear connections with the translation of matter unfamiliar to the TL audience, as we saw under the heading of presupposition, where we discussed a number of examples. The medieval practice of cutting out the boring bits in translation (Amos 1920:5), although again being a violation of the quality principle, might be a combination of politeness and relevance, while the practice of a translator from an earlier century known as Bogomolets would seem to be a violation of quantity and manner for reasons of personal self-promotion: "Where necessary, I express myself in more words, and where it is obvious that the author's language is more copious than need be, then I express the same essence in shorter form, in order not only to be compared with the author I have translated but to rise above him in liveliness of exposition" (quoted in Balcerzan 1978:124).

The application of the maxim of relevance in translation is provided in an example quoted by Ehrman (1993:165) of a 1960s translation of the sixteenth-century physician and theologian Paracelsus which omitted references to his linguistic theories because they did not match the scientific ideology of contemporary readers and were therefore not considered relevant. In this case, the maxims of quantity and quality are violated in the interests of relevance. This, just as in our examples of the maxim of quantity, is also a matter of presupposition, which shows the close imbrication of some pragmatic concepts and the difficulty sometimes of saying what precisely falls into which category.

In the English subtitles of the Mexican film *Hasta morir* (1994) there is the following exchange: *I want the pachuco with the lady. – A cholo did that for me.* This translation technique (borrowing) is a rather unusual strategy to adopt in film translation, where many people in the audience will not know the source language, since the translator is either not offering all information needed for comprehension (quantity maxim) or is not being relevant to the target audience needs (relation maxim) when they are not in a position (situation) to fill in the gaps in their knowledge (presupposition). The images on screen (context) give no indication as to what these words mean, so that the text function (ideational) is not realized and the result is incomprehension, a complete absence of clarity (manner maxim) which puts the audience in a social role of complete inferiority (register).

You might conclude that this translation is a disaster, and some of the audience would no doubt feel irritated at being left in the dark (perlocutionary act). It is also possible, however, to see this as a foreignizing translation intended to bring home the otherness of the source culture with powerful reinforcement of the interpersonal function of the text through highlighting the poetic function of language: a certain sensuous satisfaction can be derived from rolling the sounds around in the mouth and mind even if you don't know what the words mean. This last point leads to the final possibility that this translation strategy is an example of kitsch "instant exotica" (Steiner 1992:333) or "cheap local colour" (Vinay and Darbelnet 1958:53).

Whatever the reason and whatever the effect of such a translation, we can certainly say that it was not motivated by linguistics (the words are translatable) or culture (these are not specifically Mexican objects or concepts) or morality (the words are not offensive, and, in any case, the other subtitles in the film are liberally sprinkled with vulgar swear words). You might wish therefore to ask yourself whether the explanations advanced in the previous paragraph give an adequate justification for the strategy of borrowing, or whether the politeness principle would have been better served by a literal translation: in the scene in question, two friends, El Boy and Mauricio, are in a tattoo parlour. El Boy wants a tattoo just like Mauricio's: *I want the flash guy with the lady, like him*, to which Mauricio says: *A half-breed did that.*

The maxim of quality, of telling things as they are, ought to be at the very heart of translation in the concept of fidelity, and one of the hopes of a linguistic approach to translation was to produce precisely that. From a linguistic point of view, the only departures from the maxim of quality in translation should relate to those situations in which there is no linguistic expression available in the target language. This is where we enter the debate on the role in translation of gloss and exegesis, which are still linguistic operations. Even where the TL does have the means to express the source language there is still lively disagreement over the linguistic level at which translation will take place. However, as we have already indicated on many occasions, the maxim is frequently forced to yield to non-linguistic considerations, some legitimate and others not. We have already quoted Kade's belief that being a good Marxist-Leninist translator "has nothing to do with an 'ideological revaluation' as is often insinuated from the bourgeois side" (1980:46), but modern translation studies are finding examples on all sides of such interferences with 'quality' in the Gricean sense.

Equally dubious as a translation principle, at least for many modern translators, is one possible interpretation of the maxim of manner (be clear), which might imply that the translator as a text producer has the right or the duty to 'improve on' the original, as Bogomolets claimed to do. Many student translators will simply declare as axiomatic that translators have no right to improve on the original, while translators such as Niclas von Wyle believed, according to Kloepfer (1967:21), that even misprints in the original should appear in the translation.

The application of this maxim depends on who you are and what you are translating. The instruction manual for my video recorder, which is on the whole well written, nonetheless contains things like *There after* instead of *Thereafter, you video* for *your video* and *the video will build automatically know where to go*. It also at one point puts a set of instructions in the wrong paragraph. To suggest that the translator has no right to improve on this is tantamount in the first three cases to verbal foppery or casuistry and in the last case to criminal negligence and may, indeed, lead to legal proceedings being taken against the translator for damage to person and property.

With literary texts the situation is different, and the 'no improvement' maxim was probably intended to safeguard the integrity of such texts from those lesser lights who claim, for example, to have 'improved' Shakespeare. One rather bizarre form of 'improvement' was found by Hesse-Quack in the dubbing of films into German: wherever Germans are referred to negatively, the word 'German' is taken out or replaced by another nationality (1969:166).

In addition to supplying macro-level translation principles based on the Gricean maxims, implicatures will also operate at the micro-level, since it is assumed that different languages will apply the principles in different ways in different situations, and this knowledge should be part of translator competence.

An English student thought that a letter he had received from a French company was 'smarmy' when in fact it was simply written in standard politeness formulae (*I remain entirely at your disposition*, for example) of a kind which he himself had not yet learnt to use in French and which are no longer used in English, where government officials do not now *beg to remain your humble servant*. The corollary of this was that his own letters back to that company would probably have sounded quite rude. Of course, we could handle this particular concept under the heading of register rather than the politeness maxim.

In many cases translators will have no decision to make in relation to the Gricean maxims: *Isn't Jack a real pig? – The sun's come out* would presumably require no more than literal translation to preserve its implicature that Jack has just come into the room. It would, of course, be a problem in a culture (if such exists) in which bad-mouthing never happens.

At the textual level also, implicature ought not to pose problems. The most interesting part of implicatures lies in their being flouted. But on the whole, for a text to be well-written, it would tend to conform to the maxims rather than flout them. There would seem to be little point (other than ineptitude) in producing a text that rambles on in obscure irrelevance, except perhaps to signal character in a novel or as an experimental novelistic style, in which case either you would expect the translator to have little option but to follow suit, or the style in question is deemed unacceptable in the receiving culture, so translation will not be an option anyway.

This relates to the question of whether or not the maxims are universally applicable in the same way in both space and time. The boring bits which the medieval translator Aelfric cut out in translation concerned the medieval literary device of catalogue. In his *History of English Literature* Fowler tells us that "Modern readers are often put off by the extent to which older literature consists of lists; for these now seem dull and empty" (1989:3). But not just modern readers: Aelfric lived between 955 and 1020, and boredom was so feared in the seventeenth-century that the French translator Perrot d'Ablancourt devised a novel means of dealing with such lists not by wielding the axe like Aelfric but by moving them out of the main text into margins and footnotes (Rener 1989:235).

We are dealing here with the maxims of quantity and relation. If the receiving system does not use lists as a textual device they will seem over-informational and irrelevant to the TL reader. Should the translator follow the method outlined in the last paragraph (omission) or in the preceding paragraph (grin and bear it)? This is not just a question of how to translate old books; it can arise in translating modern French. The Rainbow Warrior text (Hatim and Mason 1990a:87) which we have referred to several times already contains a paragraph which is a long list, a device so unusual in English that the translators actually fall into an anacoluthon: having translated the list, which ought to be the subject of the verb, they put a dash and start the sentence off all over again, a linguistic situation they would certainly have avoided had they written the story themselves from scratch.

Similarly, the device in Russian journalism of using a transitional sentence, usually short and usually on a line of its own, such as *About what are we talking here?*, is presumably related to the maxim of manner. It clarifies textual structure by signposting. But should it be translated into a language which uses no such device?

Similar questions can be asked of the other maxims. Although much research needs to be done on how the concepts of politeness, informativity, relevance, clarity and truthfulness affect text production in different languages and different cultures, any differences that are found will raise the same question: which system is to be reflected in the translation?

12. Psycholinguistics

Psycholinguistics is about language and the mind: what goes on in the mind when we learn or use a language. Beyond proposing 'models' of the translation process, translation theorists have not been too preoccupied with the subject. More recently, however, two trends have emerged in the study of translation as a mental activity. One of these, which we shall consider second, is quite clearly a branch of psycholinguistics, since it concerns 'what goes on in the minds of translators'. The other trend, whose main proponent has been Ernst-August Gutt, is less obviously psycholinguistic but we place it here because it is based on a theory of cognition and claims to offer an ambitious account of translation purely in terms of the psychology of communication, and, more specifically, in terms of the concept of relevance.

Relevance theory

When people speak we assume they intend to pass on some kind of information. A listener has the mental capacity to infer that intention by using the linguistic properties of what the speaker says to form semantic representations in the mind. These begin as blueprints based purely on language. They need further mental processing before they can become proper thoughts that describe the world.

We get from the semantic representations to the full-fledged thought by means of context. However, in relevance theory 'context' does not mean the co-text or the situation. It is rather a set of assumptions that the listener has about the world. This set is potentially enormous, including absolutely everything the hearer can see, feel, remember, etc. To narrow it down so that we can infer speaker intention, we do two things.

First, we apply the minimax principle by activating the most easily accessible parts of context in the given situation. If we are in a train station making reservations, we are more likely to activate, and therefore have easier access to, information relevant to that situation than to any other.

Second, we will expect to benefit from any utterance in terms of improved understanding of the particular microworld we happen to be in. In the train station we expect any utterances to lead to the acquisition of tickets and information.

The principle of relevance derives directly from these two elements of effort and benefit. We choose from the context those assumptions that will satisfy two requirements:

- they will have the largest contextual effects or benefit;
- they will require least processing effort.

The hearer will take as the speaker's intention that interpretation of the speaker's utterance which conforms to this rule.

This does not necessarily make communication straightforward, because people do not always say what they think. They may exaggerate, use metaphor, or respond indirectly. This discrepancy between word and thought is accounted for by distinguishing between descriptive use and interpretive resemblance. If we say *Elizabeth I was queen of England in the sixteenth century*, we are truthfully describing the real world. If we say *If I don't get this done today, I'm dead* we are (hopefully) not truthfully describing the world. Rather our utterance interpretively resembles our thought, which will be something like 'If I don't finish this task today, my life will become very unpleasant'. The thought and the utterance have an interpretive resemblance because they share contextual implications.

Gutt applies this distinction to translation. A translation that is seen as having to relate in some way to the original would be a case of interpretive resemblance, whereas a translation intended to survive on its own without the receiver even knowing there was an original would be a case of descriptive use; it would involve whatever changes the commissioner or the translator thought necessary to maximize its effect, or relevance, for its new audience, regardless of what was in the original.

Translations of this second kind, involving descriptive use, are not really translations in Gutt's opinion. They have been called so only through loose usage or because people have found it more economical to translate an original text and modify it rather than starting a whole new text from scratch. And since they are not translations, Gutt (1991:65) believes "there will be no need for a general theory of translation to concern itself with such cases". In other words, a theory of translation has no need to bend over backwards to find concepts to accommodate and describe what are really adaptations.

Another distinction in relevance theory which is important for translation is that between primary and secondary communication situations. If the listener is to understand the speaker's informative intention, then three things must come together: the speaker's utterance, the activation of the correct set of contextual assumptions, and the properly functioning capacity to make inferences from these two things combined. When that happens, we have a primary communication situation. In some situations, however, the text receiver may fail to activate the contextual assumptions intended by the communicator. Many a spat between human beings is caused by the fact that the listener doesn't read the signs properly, or deliberately refuses to switch into the appropriate context. In that case we have a secondary communication situation, and in translation, especially between distant cultures, this is a very common occurrence.

In fact, because meaning is always inferred by reference to relevance and context, and because relevance and context change in proportion to cultural distance, Gutt (1991:99) is forced to challenge the central tenet of many translation theories: "the aim of conveying the same message does not provide a tenable basis for a general theory of translation".

This raises the question of fidelity in translation. Gutt claims that this can be defined very precisely by relevance theory, and the bulk of his book is aimed at proving this. We are told that "the principle of relevance heavily constrains the translation with regard to both what it is intended to convey and how it is expressed" (1991:101). But the only way it achieves this is by repeating the mantra: "in respects that make it adequately relevant to the audience – that is, that offer adequate contextual effects" (1991:101-102), while the manner of expression should be such "that it yields the intended interpretation without putting the audience to unnecessary processing effort" (1991:102).

With some jubilation Gutt announces that "These conditions seem to provide exactly the guidance that translators and translation theorists have been looking for: they determine in what respects the translation should resemble the original – only in those respects that can be expected to make it adequately relevant to the receptor language audience" (1991:102).

However, words such as 'adequately relevant' and 'unnecessary effort' are quite vague terms that work on a sliding scale rather than a binary opposition. This is not in itself a bad thing, but how do we find the appropriate point on the scale? Presumably by having some idea of the target audience for whom the translation is adequate and sufficiently undemanding. Newmark (1993:106) has responded to Gutt by asking "What if it [the audience] consists of the great unknown masses?", while other theorists such as Walter Benjamin believe authors write texts for themselves rather than their readers. Even specialist texts can have an astonishingly wide audience (think of Stephen Hawkings' *A Short History of Time*).

Gutt himself seems to find no problem here, admitting happily that translators may misjudge the cognitive environment of the target audience (1991:112). But this hardly amounts to providing "exactly the guidance that translators ... have been looking for" (1991:102). All Gutt can do is a retrospective analysis to explain how audiences with different degrees of knowledge will either be able to process a translation and proceed, or not process it and give up.

Gutt's next claim is that relevance theory can account for the different approaches to translation through the ages simply by saying that they were intended to maximize relevance for the contemporary audience. This is clearly right, but in that case what was the point of excluding from his theory those translation practices earlier defined as descriptive use, whose purpose was to ... maximize relevance? The clear distinction Gutt claims to have established is not that clear after all.

Gutt tries to address this problem by considering the distinction between direct and indirect quotation. In the former, we preserve the meaning and the form of expression, while in the latter we preserve only what was meant. What Gutt needs to do then is to find the translation equivalent of direct quotation. There is no straightforward answer to this because the formal means of expression vary enormously between languages, making direct formal quotation impossible. Gutt's answer is to say that it is not the intrinsic value of stylistic properties that matter but the fact that they give 'communicative clues' that guide the audience to the correct interpretation of the utterance. This seems to be not very different from Nida's view that what matters in grammar is not form but function.

Similarly, Gutt's statement that the only way of knowing whether "two utterances in language A and B share all their communicative clues is by checking whether they give rise to the same interpretation" (1991:162) is perilously close to checking for equivalent response, which he has earlier satirized.

Gutt finds himself in a situation where he has defined two forms of translation that are quite different from each other: a flexible, context-sensitive concept of translation as interpretive use with shared explicatures and implicatures and which allows for very different types of target text to be called translation; and a fixed, context-independent form of translation that preserves communicative clues. Because he has promised us a unified theory of translation, he sets out to demonstrate that direct translation is really just a special case of interpretive use.

Direct translation becomes interpretive-use translation by promising to "interpretively resemble the original completely in the context envisaged for the original" (1991:163). In the process, the concept of communicative clue, which was the subject of discussion for over thirty pages, is quietly demoted as having no "theoretical status of its own", and is reduced merely to having "some value in the practice of translation" (1991:164).

Now, direct translation can only become an example of interpretive use by building in the latter part of the definition in the preceding paragraph: the utterances have to combine with the original context for proper inferences to be made. A primary communication situation must exist, because the receiver has to be able to activate the speaker-intended context. This has two effects: first, "the need for the target audience to familiarize themselves with the context assumed by the original communicator" (1991:166); and second, the suppression of the burden on the translator to compensate for contextual mismatches by spelling out implicatures in the translation, since "in direct translation it is the audience's responsibility to make up for such differences" (1991:166). The concept of minimum processing effort for the audience seems to have disappeared from the equation, and it is left to the translator to "choose between indirect and direct translation" (1991:181) depending on what they see as relevant to the audience, and to make the decision clear to the audience in a foreword (1991:183). This is suspiciously like the choices translators had to make under the theories Gutt himself has criticized.

Having promised a unified theory of translation, what Gutt actually delivers, in an eloquent and enjoyably sharp argument, is a unified general concept that covers, while leaving intact, two completely different forms of translation.

Tirkkonen-Condit (1992:244) also argues against Gutt that translators make decisions based not on a perceived audience but on their own preferences, and that the rational minimax approach behind relevance theory may not be at all the way in which human beings behave: it may not be a true psycholinguistic concept but simply one more theoretical construct.

In other words, this is another theory about translation and translator behaviour that has been deductively arrived at from a general principle rather than inductively from empirical data. In the next section, we shall examine examples of the latter approach.

Translation strategies

Part of the problem with many of the theories of translation we have looked at so far is that their models of the process are purely theoretical constructs. They take for granted that translation takes place in stages because if you try to envisage to yourself what a translator might do, that seems a fairly logical thing to conclude. However, no one really knows what goes on inside a translator's head. And anyone who wanted to find out would have been discouraged by the prevalent scientific model which ruled that the 'black box' of the mind was inaccessible in any valid way.

Since the mid-1980s, however, researchers in Germany and Finland have increasingly taken up the methods of psychological investigation available in psycholinguistics and the cognitive sciences, applying the concepts to translation in an attempt to find out how people's minds handle the linguistic process of translating.

One of the main tools of investigation is the 'think-aloud protocol' (or TAP), in which people are asked to say whatever comes into their head while performing a task. This method of investigation is not without problems, and those researching the area spend quite some time justifying the procedure itself and the target groups it is used on. However, the methodological problems are of less interest to us here than the results.

Krings (1986:260-62) studied the strategies his subjects (advanced language learners) used in the comprehension, translation and evaluation stages of the translation process. He found that in the comprehension (reception) phase of translating they had massive recourse to dictionaries for solving problems; only in a quarter of problem situations did they use their problem-solving ability by making their own inferences. In 75% of cases the use of the bilingual dictionary did actually lead to the right answer, compared with only 40% right answers arrived at by making inferences from the context.

In the translation phase, Krings again finds considerable reliance on the bilingual dictionary. If the dictionary offered only one translation, the subjects used it without any further thought. Where two or more equivalents were offered, the main concern of the subjects became that of checking to see which one would fit into the immediate syntactic context, even if they did not understand the equivalent they had chosen. Krings comments, "At least in some cases the subjects are aware that they are translating without understanding" (1986:393). In most cases the subjects (presumably because of the way they had learned the foreign language) were able to associate only one target equivalent with the source unit, and in most cases they solved the problem of finding an equivalent at no higher than the word level (1986:399).

In the evaluation and decision-making stage (1986:464-67) the subjects finalized the choice of equivalent by using two main strategies: 'playing-it-safe' reduction strategies in which the target message underwent a loss in relation to the source, and 'risk-taking' achievement strategies in which the subjects attempted to provide a full translation without knowing if the solutions offered were right or not. Where various possible solutions had to be weighed up, the subjects' choice tended to be guided by 'translation maxims'. Krings found seven of these (1986:429-34):

(i)   Literalism maxim: avoid translations that move too far away from the source text;
(ii) Length-restriction maxim: one subject rejected an 'overlong' translation citing the 'rule' of an authority on translation that 'a translation should never be more than 10% longer than the original' (1986:430);
(iii) Translational constancy maxim: the notion that a given source unit should always be translated by the same target-language word(s);

(iv) Variety maxim: the idea that different source units must be translated by different target units rather than being allowed to converge into the same word;

(v) Foreign-word maxim: when in doubt use a 'proper' target-language word rather than a similar-sounding loan word (a constant problem in German where so many English words have been imported and where, even though these loan words are used with considerable frequency by native German writers, student translators are told to avoid them);

(vi) Corrective maxim: where translators find, or think they have found, an error in the source text, some will correct it in translation while others will insist that you should not 'improve' on the original in any way whatsoever;

(vii) Translator-tools maxim: this takes us into the realm of the light fantastic; Krings found that his translators followed such maxims as:

- never translate a source-language word you don't know by a target-language word that isn't in the dictionary;
- trust the dictionary even when you don't understand it;
- when in doubt, take the first word offered in the dictionary list of equivalents.

Another German scholar who has researched what seems to go on in the minds of translators is Lörscher. Like Krings, Lörscher worked not with professional translators but with students. This means his subjects faced problems of a kind not faced by professionals (less knowledge of the foreign language and culture, hence the need to make massive use of the dictionary) but they did *not* face problems of a kind that professional translators do have to deal with (carrying out research and taking account of customer requirements, for example). Both authors also studied translation into the foreign language, which, although it does happen, is not recommended as best practice in the professional world of translation. Consequently the results of these studies may tell us more about language-learning needs than about translation strategies.

Lörscher (1991:280) counters this by suggesting that what such studies reveal are not specifically translation activities but rather general strategies for processing texts. In any event, Kussmaul and Tirkkonen-Condit (1995:181) quote research by Jääskeläinen and Tirkkonen-Condit to the effect that using professional translators for think-aloud-protocols is counter-productive, since subjects tend to fall silent when the task in hand is so routine that it requires little effort, and for professional translators this will happen a lot.

Lörscher's study aims to find out what range of strategies translators use, how frequently they occur, what kinds of problems they are able to solve, and how successful they are.

From the mass of data, Lörscher (1991:97-117) has uncovered five basic translation strategies built out of twenty-two elements. These basic strategies may contain embedded elements within the chain and bound elements at the end. These are not part of the attempt to solve the problem but probably play a psychological role of mental succour. The basic strategies can be made into expanded structures by adding in further elements that are part of the problem-solving process, and they can be built into complex structures by putting together one or more basic strategies. The elements that go to produce the basic structures include:

- realizing the existence of a translation problem;
- verbalizing the problem;
- searching for a solution;
- finding a definitive or temporary, whole or part solution;
- putting off the search for a solution;
- failing to find a solution;
- having a problem in understanding the source text.

These elements occur exclusively within what Lörscher calls 'strategic' phases of the translation process, in other words those parts of translating in which a problem is being specifically addressed.

The further set of elements may or may not occur in such phases. The list of these elements is too long to quote in full, but they involve such mental activities as repeating or rephrasing the source and target language texts, checking a possible solution against the source text or against the target context, mentally organizing a source-text segment to find a starting point or to translate it as a whole rather than word by word, commenting on the text or commenting on what the translator is actually doing.

Out of these elements, the basic translation strategies are built up. These are actually quite simple, ranging from the straightforward:

Realize there is a problem + Solve it or Fail to solve it for the time being

to the more complicated:

Realize there is a problem + Search for a solution + Verbalize part of the problem + Solve that part or put it off + Search for a solution to the next part, etc.

In other words, the strategies build up through the addition of extra stages in verbalizing and searching for solutions to all or part of the problem. Embedded within or appended to the end of the strategies will be the elements of monitoring, rephrasing, checking and so on.

The actual translation results produced by these strategies show that Lörscher's subjects, like those of Krings and probably for the same reason, tend to have just one-to-one associations between the source and the target translation units. This means they tend to produce sign-oriented rather than sense-oriented translations; their translation unit is the formal linguistic sign rather than the sense of the message. Where such an approach produces nonsense, the subjects are often not even aware of it because they rarely check their translations to make sure they make sense (1991:272-73), even though experiment shows that they have usually correctly understood the original text (1991:276).

As translators become more experienced and acquire greater control over their mother tongue, so the translation strategy moves more toward the sense-oriented approach based on larger translation units with checking for style and text typology (Kussmaul and Tirkkonen-Condit 1995:187). Tirkkonen-Condit has found that the more professional translators also make better use of the minimax strategy, allowing wider goals to influence local decision-making and prioritizing tasks so that they make better use of world knowledge and inferencing capacities rather than having constant and time-wasting recourse to dictionaries. As she says, "Since time is a limited resource, a good translator does not necessarily aim at an optimal perform-ance but at a performance which is sufficient in a given communicative situation" (Kussmaul and Tirkkonen-Condit 1995:190).

This probably means professionals make better use of what is called top-down processing, working from general concepts and objectives down to precise goals, rather than bottom-up processing, working from data, which, in translation, means the specific words on the page. This would seem to be supported by Janet Fraser (1996:88-89), whose research shows the influence of a specific translation brief on the thought processes and translation outcomes of professional translators. An entire issue of *Meta* (vol. 47, no. 1) is devoted to this topic of translation processes and would make an appropriate starting place for those interested in pursuing the matter.

This research would suggest that trainee translators and experienced translators behave rather differently. What is not yet known is how they get from one to the other. One way of finding out might be to pursue Brian Harris's proposal (1992) to go even further back down the translation chain to look at what he calls 'natural' translation, which is translation done in daily life by bilingual children with no training as translators. Such research is still in its infancy and not accepted by everybody, but it may yet have a contribution to make to unravelling the mystery of translation.

Conclusion and Perspectives

Translation can be addressed by a number of discourses. The late Antoine Berman (1989) has categorized these as:

* objective sectorial, in which translation is seen as an object of study for specific disciplines such as linguistics, poetics or comparative literature;
* objective general, where translation becomes the object of general discourse studies such as hermeneutics;
* experiential, which intertwines translation and philosophy or psychoanalysis.

Berman (1989:673) has the following to say about the linguistic discourse on translation studies: linguistics continues to insist that translation is a proper object of linguistic study, and provides a conceptual analytical framework for that study, but defines translation in such an abstract way that it ignores almost entirely the written and textual aspects of the act, not to mention its cultural and historical dimensions. He attributes this to the fact that theoretical linguists have no real interest in translation studies.

This is not entirely true, as I hope to have demonstrated. Yet this lack of interest, where it exists, may be attributed to the highly abstract formalism of much of modern linguistics which has nothing obvious to do with the messy reality of language in use. This could be one reason why some translation theorists view linguistics as a positivist discourse of patriarchal repression seeking to shackle everything to system and structure.

Some linguists' lack of interest might also be due to despair. As I have suggested throughout, although translation phenomena may be amenable to linguistic description, linguistics is not necessarily the discipline which guides us to the 'right' answers, which allows us to pick our way through the imbrication of what Barbara Folkart (1989:149) has called the *ratio facilis* of translation, the appropriation of an idiom, and the *ratio difficilis*, the invention of an idiolect, an imbrication and a dialectic not readily amenable to the cut-and-dried categorizations that linguistics strives for.

Translation is a site of tension and conflict, an activity swept along, in the dark and without a reliable compass, on the currents of culture, ideology and history. The theories we construct, our whistling in the dark, are intended to give some direction to the flow and some comfort to the navigator. The linguistic discourse is just one of those theories and cannot completely circumscribe translation, and yet, as the continued proliferation of research demonstrates, it has a role to play and a voice which will not be silenced.

Earlier linguistic theories of translation fell mainly within the domain of contrastive linguistics, which is not the same as a translation linguistics but still an important element of translation studies. Without systemic comparisons you have no basis for discussion. But the comparisons need to be, and have been, extended beyond the confines of differential semantics and grammar into the broader areas of text structure and functioning, into the sociocultural functioning of translation and how it is shaped and constrained by the place and time in which it takes place. In all of this, linguistics will have a part to play.

Glossary

Adaptation: replacing source-language cultural items by target-language equivalents. See pp. 39-40.

Amplification: **1.** (Vinay and Darbelnet): characteristic of a language that expresses itself more verbosely than another language. **2.** (Malone) adding information to allow the reader of a translation to understand the text. See pp. 45-47.

Anacoluthon: wrongful mixing of grammatical structures. See p. 93.

Anaphora: referring back to some earlier item in a text. See p. 95.

Antonymic Translation (Shveitser): translating by an antonym with appropriate modifications. See p. 31.

Borrowing: transferring a source language item into the target language to fill a lexical gap or to give local colour. Called 'Carry-Over Matching' by Malone. See pp. 34-35, 42.

Calque (Loan Translation): borrowing a source language item in translated form. See pp. 35-36.

Cataphora: referring forward to an item that comes at a later point in the text. See p. 95.

Coherence: conceptual connectedness of a text. See pp. 98-99.

Cohesion: lexico-grammatical connectedness of a text. See pp. 90-98.

Collocation: set phrase, words that typically go together. See pp. 6-8.

Communicative Translation (Newmark): attempts to maintain the effect of the original. See p. 114.

Compensation: manipulating one part of a text to make up for a loss in another. See pp. 31-33.

Concentration (Vinay and Darbelnet): translating with fewer words without loss of meaning. Called 'Condensation' by Malone. See pp. 47-49.

Concretization (Shveitser): translating an abstract by a concrete term. See pp. 29-30.

Connotation: the 'peripheral', non-denotational meanings of a word. See pp. 23-25.

Convergence (Malone): translating different source words by one target word. See pp. 43-45.

Conversational Maxims: principles governing conversational cooperation. Seenpp. 130-134.

Covert Translation (House): one which is not obviously a translation. See p. 113.

Cultural Translation (Nida): changing source content to conform to the target culture. See p. 58.

Deconstruction: reading a text by seizing on apparently peripheral matter in order to bring out the concealed 'violent hierarchy' of its dominant ideological values; the philosophy that no text has a fixed and stable meaning. See pp. 16, 72, 108.

Deixis: words like *this*, *now*, *here*, etc. which locate things in time and space. See pp. 94-95.

Denotational Meaning: what the word refers to in the real world, or its dictionary definition in the case of abstract words. See p. 6, 23-24.

Differentiation (Shveitser): translating a general term by a more specific term. See pp. 29-30.

Dilution (Vinay and Darbelnet): translating with more words but without addition of meaning. Called 'Diffusion' by Malone. See pp. 47-49.

Directive Function: language used to influence behaviour. See p. 102.

Divergence (Malone): translating one source word by more than one target word in different contexts. See pp. 43-45.

Documentary Translation (Nord): translation strategy for texts not intended for the target-language audience. See p. 114.

Dynamic Equivalence (Nida): eliciting the same reader response as the original. See pp. 56-60.

Economy (Vinay and Darbelnet): characteristic of a language that expresses itself more concisely than another language. See p. 47.

Equation (Malone): literal translation involving only necessary grammatical changes. See pp. 41-43.

Équivalence (Vinay and Darbelnet): translating idioms, collocations, proverbs, etc. by the natural target equivalent. See pp. 38-39.

Equivalence: relation between a source text and its translation usually intended to mean that the target unit is as close as possible in meaning to the source unit while still being natural usage in the target language. See Chapter 5.

Equivalent Translation (Kade): performs the same function as the original. See p. 112.

Explicitation Hypothesis: phenomenon whereby a translated text is usually more explicit, both in the expression of grammatical links and of semantic content, than the original. See p. 100.

Expressive Function: **1.** language used to express the feelings of the speaking subject; **2.** language in which the formal properties are at least as important as their meaning. See p. 101.

Faux-amis: source and target language words that look alike but have different meanings. See p. 43.

Foreignizing Translation: makes the target text 'alien' in order to convey the Otherness of the source culture. See p. 116.

Formal Correspondence (Nida and Catford): translation that adheres closely to the linguistic form of the source text. See p. 54.

Functional Sentence Perspective: the semantics of sentence structure. See p. 85.

Generalization (Shveitser): translating a more specific source-language item by a more general target-language item. See pp. 29-30.

Heterovalent Translation (Kade): performs a different function from the original. See p. 112.

Hypernym: a more general word embracing several more specific terms. See p. 20.

Hyponym: a word whose meaning is included in that of a more general word. See p. 20.

Ideational Function: language used to convey information, ideas or experience. See pp. 108-109.

Instrumental Translation (Nord): translation strategy for texts aimed equally at a source and target language audience. See p. 114.

Interpersonal Function: language used to establish a relationship between author and reader. See pp. 109-110.

Kernel: the most basic syntactic representation of a sentence in its deep structure. See pp. 65-67.

Langue: language as an abstract rule system. See pp. 3-4.

Lexicalization: expressing a concept in compact lexical form. See p. 16.

Linguistic Translation (Nida): makes explicit only information that is linguistically implicit in the original. See p. 58.

Literal Translation: **1.** translation strategy in which the whole text is subjected to translation at a low linguistic level; **2.** translation technique in which parts of a text are translated at a low level because the results conform to target language norms. See pp. 36, 112-113.

Matching (Malone): generic term for 'Substitution' and 'Equation' (q.v.). See pp. 41-43.

Metalinguistic Function: the use of language to talk about language. See p. 101.

Minimax Principle: seeking maximum effect or benefit for minimum effort. See p. 12.

Mood: grammatical structuring of the clause into sentence types to convey interpersonal meaning. See p. 109.

Modulation (Vinay and Darbelnet): modifying the semantics of the source term to produce a target equivalent. See pp. 37-38.

Morpheme: smallest linguistic unit of meaning. See pp. 14-17.

Natural Translation: spontaneous, untutored translation of young bilingual speakers. See p. 143.

Overt Translation (House): one which is visibly a translation. See p. 113.

Paradigmatic: the structuring of language on the 'vertical' dimension whereby a slot in a linguistic chain can be filled by items taken from the same grammatical or semantic set. See pp. 6-7.

Parole: language in actual use. See pp. 3-4.

Phatic Function: language used to maintain contact between speaker and listener. See p. 102.

Prefabricated Matching (Malone): translating by a conventionalized linguistic routine. See p. 42.

Presupposition: knowledge that a reader is assumed to have already on coming to a text. See pp. 123-126.

Recrescence (Malone): generic term for 'amplification' and 'reduction' (q.v.). See pp. 45-47.

Reduction (Malone): omitting information that is not needed or will be misunderstood. See p. 47.

Redundancy: repetition in utterances to counteract interference or avoid a high load of new information. See p. 57.

Referential: see 'Denotational' and 'Ideational'.

Register: variations in language dictated by the interaction of language user (located in time, space and society) and language use (field, mode, tenor). See pp. 75-84.

Re-ordering (Malone): altering the position of sentence constituents. See pp. 49-50.

Repackaging (Malone): generic term for 'diffusion' and 'condensation' (q.v.). See pp. 47-49.

Restricted Translation (Catford): translates only one level of the source text. See p. 56.

Rheme: that part of the clause which provides new information to develop the theme. See pp. 85-90.

Scenes and Frames: a form of semantics that sees words as frames which conjure up mental scenes. The French *steak-frites* and the English *fish and chips* are frames that activate the same scene of 'basic everyday meal'. See pp. 98-99.

Skopos theory: says that translation strategy is determined by the function of the translated text, which may not be the same as that of the original. See p. 72.

Selection Restrictions: elements of a word's meaning that allow it to form collocations with some words but not others. See p. 7.

Semantic Translation (Newmark): remains as close as possible to the lexico-grammatical structures of the original. See p. 114.

Substitution (Malone): a form of dynamic equivalence used when literal translation (equation) is not possible and so some form of translation shift must take place. See p. 41.

Syntagmatic: structuring of language along the horizontal level. See pp. 6-7.

Taxonomy: a classification or conceptual structuring of a subject. See p. 26.

Textual Equivalence (Catford): target-language text segment that can be observed to be the equivalent of a source-language text segment. See pp. 54-56.

Theme: that part of a sentence that announces what it is going to be about. See ppp. 85-90.

Transitivity: conceptual organization of the clause to express the ideational function. See p. 109.

Translation Shift: any departure from formal correspondence in translation. See p. 51.

Transposition (Vinay and Darbelnet): shifts of grammar and syntax in translation. See p. 37.

Zigzagging (Malone): generic term for divergence and convergence (q.v.). See pp. 43-45.

Bibliography

Albrecht, Jörn (1973) *Linguistik und Übersetzung*, Tübingen: Niemeyer.

Amos, Flora Ross (1920) *Early Theories of Translation*, New York: Octagon Books; reprinted 1973.

Andrews, Avery (1985) 'The Major Functions of the Noun Phrase', in Timothy Shopen (ed) *Language Typology and Syntactic Description*, Vol. I, Cambridge: Cambridge University Press, 62-154.

Baker, Mona (1992) *In Other Words: A Coursebook on Translation*, London & New York: Routledge.

Baker, Mona (1993) 'Corpus Linguistics and Translation Studies: Implications and Applications', in Mona Baker, Gill Francis and Elena Tognini-Bonelli (eds) *Text and Technology: In Honour of John Sinclair*, Amsterdam & Philadelphia: John Benjamins, 233-50.

Balcerzan, Edward (1978) 'Perevod kak tvorchestvo' (Translation as Creation), *Babel* 21(3): 124-26.

Bassnett-Maguire, Susan (1980) *Translation Studies*, London: Methuen; revised edition 1993.

Bassnett, Susan and André Lefevere (eds) (1990) *Translation, History and Culture*, London & New York: Pinter Publishers.

Beaugrande, Robert de and Wolfgang Dressler (1981) *Introduction to Text Linguistics*, London & New York: Longman.

Bell, Roger T. (1991) *Translation and Translating. Theory and Practice*, London: Longman.

Benjamin, Andrew (1989) *Translation and the Nature of Philosophy*, London & New York: Routledge.

Berman, Antoine (1989) 'La traduction et ses discours', *Meta* 34(4): 672-79.

Blum-Kulka, Shoshana (1986) 'Shifts of Cohesion and Coherence in Translation', in Juliane House and Shoshana Blum-Kulka (eds) *Interlingual and Intercultural Communication*, Tübingen: Gunter Narr, 17-35.

Broek, Raymond van den (1978) 'The Concept of Equivalence in Translation Theory: Some Critical Reflections', in James S. Holmes, José Lambert and Raymond van den Broek (eds) *Literature and Translation: New Perspectives in Literary Studies*, Leuven: Acco, 29-43.

Burgess, Anthony (1962) *A Clockwork Orange*, London: Heinemann.

Cary, Edmond (1957) 'Théories soviétiques de la traduction', *Babel* 3(4): 179-90.

Catford, John C. (1965) *A Linguistic Theory of Translation*, London: Oxford University Press.

Chapdelaine, Annick (1994) 'Transparence et retraduction des sociolectes dans *The Hamlet* de Faulkner', *TTR* 7(2): 11-33.

Cherniakhovskaia, Leonora. A. (1977) 'Sinnstruktur und syntaktische Umformung beim Übersetzen', in Otto Kade (ed) *Vermittelte Kommunikation, Sprachmittlung, Translation*, Leipzig: VEB Verlag Enzyklopädie, 86-92.

Chomsky, Noam (1965) *Aspects of the Theory of Syntax*, Cambridge, MA: The MIT Press.

Chuquet, Hélène and Michel Paillard (1987) *Approche linguistique des problèmes de la traduction: anglais-français*, Paris: Ophrys.

Comrie, Bernard (1979) 'Russian', in Timothy Shopen (ed) *Languages and their Status*, Cambridge, Mass.: Winthrop Publishers.

Crystal, David and Derek Davy (1969) *Investigating English Style*, London: Longman.

Delisle, Jean (1988) *Translation: an Interpretive Approach*, Ottawa: University of Ottawa Press.

Diaz-Diocaretz, Myriam (1985) *Translating Poetic Discourse: Questions on Feminist Strategies in Adrienne Rich*, Amsterdam: John Benjamins.

Duff, Alan (1981) *The Third Language: Recurrent Problems of Translation into English*, Oxford: Pergamon Press.

Durieux, Christine (1990) 'La recherche documentaire en traduction technique: conditions nécessaires et suffisantes', *Meta* 35(4): 669-75.

Eggins, Suzanne (1994) *An Introduction to Systemic Functional Linguistics*, London & New York: Pinter Publishers.

Ehrman, James F. (1993) 'Pragmatics and Translation: The Problem of Presupposition', *TTR* 6(1): 149-70.

Faiss, Klaus (1973) 'Übersetzung und Sprachwissenschaft – eine Orientierung', *Babel* 19(2): 75-86.

Fedorov, Andrei V. (1953) *Vvedenie v teoriu perevoda* (Introduction to the Theory of Translation), Moscow: Literaturi na inostrannix iazikax; 2nd revised edition 1958; 3rd revised edition 1968: *Osnovy obshchei teorii perevoda* (Foundations of a General Theory of Translation), Moscow: Visshaia shkola.

Foley, William A. and Robert D. Van Valin, Jr. (1985) 'Information Packaging in the Clause', in Timothy Shopen (ed) *Language Typology and Syntactic Description*, Cambridge: Cambridge University Press, 282-364.

Folkart, Barbara (1989) 'La matérialité du texte: la traduction comme récupération de l'intra-discursif', *Meta* 34(2): 143-56.

Fowler, Alastair (1989) *A History of English Literature*, Oxford: Basil Blackwell.

Fraser, Janet (1996) 'Mapping the Process of Translation', *Meta* 47(1): 84-96.

Gak, Vladimir G. (1992) 'Pour un calcul logique des équivalents de traduction', *Meta* 37(1): 139-48.

Gallagher, John D. (1993) 'The Quest for Equivalence', *Lebende Sprachen* 38(4): 150-61.

Gentzler, Edwin (1993) *Contemporary Translation Theories*, London & New York: Routledge.

Gerrard, Nicci (1996) 'Nam's Inhumanity to Man', *The Observer: Books*, 21 January, p. 15.

Govaert, Marcel (1971) 'Critères de traduction', in Karl-Richard Bausch and Hans Martin Geiger (eds) *Interlinguistica. Sprachvergleich und Übersetzung. Festschrift zum 60. Geburtstag von Mario Wandruszka*, Tübingen: Max Niemeyer, 425-37.

Grice, H. Paul (1975) 'Logic and Conversation', in Peter Cole and Jerry L. Morgan (eds) *Syntax and Semantics, Vol. III: Speech Acts*, New York: Academic Press, 41-58.

Gutt, Ernst-August (1991) *Translation and Relevance: Cognition and Context*, Oxford: Blackwell.

Güttinger, Fritz (1963) *Zielsprache. Theorie und Technik der Übersetzung*, Zürich: Manesse.

Hamblin, Charles (1990) *Languages of Asia and the Pacific*, North Ryde (Australia): Collins/Angus & Robertson.

Harris, Brian (1992) 'Natural Translation: A Reply to Hans P. Krings', *Target* 4(1): 97-103.

Hatim, Basil and Ian Mason (1990a) *Discourse and the Translator*, London: Longman.

Hatim, Basil and Ian Mason (1990b) 'Genre, Discourse and Text in the Critique of Translation', *Bradford Occasional Papers*, No. 10: 1-13.

Hatim, Basil and Ian Mason (1997) *The Translator as Communicator*, London & New York: Routledge.

Hawkins, John A. (1986) *A Comparative Typology of English and German: Unifying the Contrasts*, London & Sydney: Croom Helm.

Heidegger, Martin (1962) *Being and Time*, translated by John Macquarrie and Edward Robinson, London: S.C.M. Press.

Herbst, Thomas (1994) *Linguistische Aspekte der Synchronisation von Fernsehserien: Phonetik, Textlinguistik, Übersetzungstheorie*, Tübingen: Niemeyer.

Hesse-Quack, Otto (1969) *Der Übertragungsprozeß bei der Synchronisation von Filmen. Eine interkulturelle Untersuchung*, Munich & Basel: Ernst Reinhard.

Hickey, Leo (1993) 'Presupposition Under Cross-Examination', *International Journal for the Semiotics of Law* 6(16): 89-109.

Hines, Barry (1968) *Kes*, Harmondsworth: Penguin Books, translated into French by Lola Tranec-Dubled, Paris: Gallimard, 1968.

Hjort, Anne Mette (1990) 'Translation and the Consequences of Scepticism', in Susan Bassnett and André Lefevere (eds) *Translation, History and Culture*, London & New York: Pinter Publishers, 38-45.

Hockett, Charles (1958) *A Course in Modern Linguistics*, New York: Macmillan.

Høeg, Peter (1992) *Miss Smilla's Feeling for Snow*, translated by F. David, London: HarperCollins (Flamingo), 1993.

Holmes, Janet (1992) *An Introduction to Sociolinguistics*, London & New York: Longman.

Holz-Mänttäri, Justa (1984) *Translatorisches Handeln: Theorie und Methode*, Helsinki: Suomalainen Tiedeakatemia.

Hönig, Hans G. and Paul Kussmaul (1984) *Strategie der Übersetzung: Ein Lehr- und Arbeitsbuch*, Tübingen: Gunter Narr.

House, Juliane (1977) *A Model for Translation Quality Assessment*, Tübingen: Gunter Narr.

Hu, Qian (1994) 'On the Implausibility of Equivalent Response (Part V)', *Meta* 39(3): 418-32.

Ireland, Jeanette (1989) 'Ideology, Myth and the Maintenance of Cultural Identity', *ELR Journal* 3: 95-136.

Ivir, Vladimir (1996) 'A Case for Linguistics in Translation Theory', *Target* 8(1): 149-57.

James, Carl (1980) *Contrastive Analysis*, London: Longman.

Jumpelt, Rudolf Walter (1961) *Die Übersetzung naturwissenschaftlicher und technischer Literatur*, Berlin: Langenscheidt.

Kade, Otto (ed) (1977) *Vermittelte Kommunikation, Sprachmittlung, Translation*, Leipzig: VEB Verlag Enzyklopädie.

Kade, Otto (1980) *Die Sprachmittlung als gesellschaftliche Erscheinung und Gegenstand wissenschaftlicher Untersuchung*, Leipzig: VEB Verlag Enzyklopädie.

Keller, Adelbert von (ed) (1861) *Translationen von Niclas von Wyle*, Stuttgart: Stuttgart Verein No. 57; reprinted 1967, Hildesheim: G. Olms.

Kemp, Arnold (1996) 'Shadow of Sleaze Dims City of Light', *The Observer*, 15 December, p. 11.

Kelly, Louis (1979) *The True Interpreter. A History of Translation Theory and Practice in the West*, Oxford: Basil Blackwell.

Kloepfer, Rolf (1967) *Die Theorie der literarischen Übersetzung*, Munich: Wilhelm Fink.

Koller, Werner (1979) *Einführung in die Übersetzungswissenschaft*, Heidelberg: Quelle & Meyer.

Komissarov, Vilen N. (1977) 'Zur Theorie der linguistischen Übersetzungsanalyse', in Otto Kade (ed) *Vermittelte Kommunikation, Sprachmittlung, Translation*, Leipzig: VEB, 44-51.

Krings, Hans P. (1986) *Was in den Köpfen von Übersetzern vorgeht. Eine empirische Untersuchung zur Struktur des Übersetzungsprozesses an fortgeschrittenen Französischlernern*, Tübingen: Gunter Narr.

Kuhiwczak, Piotr (1990) 'Translation as Appropriation: The Case of Milan Kundera's *The Joke*', in Susan Bassnett and André Lefevere (eds) *Translation, History and Culture*, London & New York: Routledge, 118-30.

Kussmaul, Paul (1995) *Training the Translator*, Amsterdam & Philadelphia: John Benjamins.

Kussmaul, Paul and Sonja Tirkkonen-Condit (1995) 'Think-Aloud Protocol Analysis in Translation Studies', *TTR* 8(1): 177-99.

Ladmiral, Jean-René (1979) *Traduire: théorèmes pour la traduction*, Paris: Payot.

Larose, Robert (1989) *Théories contemporaines de la traduction*, 2nd edition, Québec: Presses de l'Université de Québec.

Lauder, Afferbeck (1968) *Fraffly Well Spoken: How to Speak the Language of London's West End*, London: Wolfe.

Lederer, Marianne (1994) *La traduction aujourd'hui*, Paris: Hachette.

Leech, Geoffrey (1981) *Semantics: The Study of Meaning*, Harmondsworth: Penguin Books.

Leuven-Zwart, Kitty van (1989) 'Translation and Original: Similarities and Dissimilarities, 1', *Target* 1(2): 151-81.

Leuven-Zwart, Kitty van (1990) 'Translation and Original: Similarities and Dissimilarities, 2', *Target* 2(1): 69-95.

Levý, Jiří (1967) 'Translation as a Decision Process', *To Honor Roman Jakobson: Essays on the Occasion of his 70th Birthday*, Vol. 2, The Hague: Mouton, 1171-82.

Levý, Jiří (1969) *Die literarische Übersetzung. Theorie einer Kunstgattung*, Frankfurt & Bonn: Athenäum; originally published 1963 as *Uměni Překladu*.

London, John (1990) '*Theatrical Poison*: Translating for the Stage', *Bradford Occasional Papers*, No. 10: 141-67.

Lörscher, Wolfgang (1991) *Translation Performance, Translation Process, and Translation Strategies. A Psycholinguistic Investigation*, Tübingen: Gunter Narr.

MacErlean, Neasa (1996) 'Tipping the Scales is not a Tip for the Top', *The Observer: Business*, 15 December, p. 9.

Malblanc, André (1963) *Stylistique comparée du français et de l'allemand: Essai de représentation linguistique comparée et étude de traduction*, Paris: Didier.

Malone, Joseph L. (1988) *The Science of Linguistics in the Art of Translation: Some Tools from Linguistics for the Analysis and Practice of Translation*, Albany: State University of New York Press.

Mel'čuk, Igor A. (1978) 'Théorie de langage, théorie de traduction', *Meta* 24(4): 271-302.

Meschonnic, Henri (1986) 'Alors la traduction chantera', *Revue d'esthétique*, New series, No. 12: 75-90.

Motion, Andrew (1995) 'When Pushkin Comes to Shove or Love', *The Observer: Books*, 8 January, p. 20.

Mounin, Georges (1963) *Les problèmes théoriques de la traduction*, Paris: Gallimard.

Neubert, Albrecht (1978) 'Pragmaticheskie Aspekti Perevoda' (Pragmatic Aspects of Translation), in Vilen N. Komissarov (ed) *Voprosi Teorii Perevoda v zarubezhnoi lingvistike* (Questions of the Theory of Translation in Foreign Linguistics), Moscow: Mezhdunarodnie otnositelia, 185-202; originally published 1968 in *Fremdsprachen: Grundfragen der Übersetzungswissenschaft* 2: 21-33.

Neubert, Albrecht (1977) 'Übersetzungswissenschaft in soziolinguistischer Sicht', in Otto Kade (ed) *Vermittelte Kommunikation, Sprachmittlung, Translation,* Leipzig: VEB, 52-59.

Newmark, Peter (1981) *Approaches to Translation,* Oxford: Pergamon.

Newmark, Peter (1993) *Paragraphs on Translation,* Clevedon: Multilingual Matters.

Newmark, Peter (1996) 'Paragraphs on Translation – 43', *The Linguist* 35(3): 90-93.

Nida, Eugene A. (1964) *Toward a Science of Translating,* Leiden: E. J. Brill.

Nida, Eugene A. and Charles R. Taber (1969) *The Theory and Practice of Translation,* Leiden: E. J. Brill; reprinted 1974.

Nord, Christiane (1991) *Text Analysis in Translation. Theory, Methodology, and Didactic Applications of a Model for Translation-Oriented Text Analysis,* Amsterdam: Rodopi.

Nord, Christiane (1995) 'Text-Functions in Translation: Titles and Headings as a Case in Point', *Target* 7(2): 261-84.

Osgood, Charles E., George J. Suci and Percy H. Tannenbaum (1957) *The Measurement of Meaning,* Urbana: University of Illinois Press; 2nd edition 1967.

Palmer, Frank R. (1981) *Semantics,* Cambridge: Cambridge University Press.

Pergnier, Maurice (1993) *Les fondements sociolinguistiques de la traduction,* Lille: Presses universitaires de Lille.

Popovič, Anton and Imrich Dénes (1977) *Translation as Comparison,* Nitra: KLKEM.

Pratchett, Terry (1989) *Pyramids,* London: Corgi.

Rabassa, Gregory (1984) 'If This be Treason: Translation and its Possibilities', in William Frawley (ed) *Translation: Literary, Linguistic and Philosophical Perspectives,* Newmark: University of Delaware Press and London & Toronto: Associated University Presses.

Radó, György (1979) 'Outline of a Systematic Translatology', *Babel* 25(4): 187-96.

Reiss, Katharina (1971) *Möglichkeiten und Grenzen der Übersetzungskritik,* Munich: Max Hueber.

Reiss, Katharina (1976) *Texttyp und Übersetzungsmethode: Der operative Text,* Kronberg: Scriptor.

Reiss, Katharina and Hans J. Vermeer (1984) *Grundlegung einer allgemeinen Translationstheorie,* Tübingen: Niemeyer.

Rener, Frederick M. (1989) *Interpretatio: Language and Translation from Cicero to Tytler*, Amsterdam: Rodopi.

Retsker, Yakob I. (1974) *Teoria perevoda i perevodcheskaia praktika* (Theory of Translation and Translation Practice), Moscow: Mezhdunarodnii otnoshenia.

Richards, Ivor A. (1953) 'Toward a Theory of Translation', in Arthur F. Wright (ed) *Studies in Chinese Thought*, Chicago: University of Chicago Press, 147-62.

Robinson, Douglas (1991) *The Translator's Turn*, Baltimore & London: The John Hopkins University Press.

Romney, Jonathan (1996) 'The pain in Spain', *The Observer: Books*, 21 January, p. 15.

Ross, Nigel J. (1995) 'Dubbing American in Italy', *English Today* 41(1): 45-48.

Sa'Adeddin, Mohammed A.A.M. (1990) 'Towards a Viable Applied Linguistic Theory of Translation: An Ethnolinguistic Point of View', *Bradford Occasional Papers*, No. 10: 14-45.

Sadock, Jerrold M. and Arnold M. Zwicky (1985) 'Speech Act Distinctions in Syntax', in Timothy Shopen (ed) *Language Typology and Syntactic Description*, Cambridge: Cambridge University Press, 155-96.

Samuelson, Paul A. (1970) *Economics*, Vol. 1, New York: McGraw Hill, 8th edition; translated into French by G. Fain as *L'Economique: Introduction à l'analyse économique*, Paris: Armand Colin, 1972, and into German by U. Schlieper as *Volkswirtschaftslehre: Eine Einführung*, Cologne: Bund-Verlag, 1973.

Saussure, Ferdinand de (1972) *Cours de linguistique générale*, Paris: Payot; originally published 1916.

Schleiermacher, Friedrich (1838) 'Über die verschiedenen Methoden des Übersetzens', in Hans Joachim Störig (ed) *Das Problem des Übersetzens*, Darmstadt: Wissenschaftliche Buchgesellschaft, 1963, 38-70.

Searle, John R. (1975) 'Indirect Speech Acts', in Peter Cole and Jerry L. Morgan (eds) *Syntax and Semantics, Vol. III: Speech Acts*, New York: Academic Press, 59-82.

Shveitser, Aleksandr D. (1977) 'Übersetzung und Soziolinguistik', in O. Kade (ed) *Vermittelte Kommunikation, Sprachmittlung, Translation*, Leipzig: VEB, 60-65.

Shveitser, Aleksandr D. (1987) *Übersetzung und Linguistik*, Berlin: Akademie; original title *Perevod i Lingvistika*, 1973.

Shveitser, Aleksandr D. (1988) *Teoria perevoda i ustniy perevod: status, problemy, aspekty* (Theory of Translation and Interpreting: Status, Problems, Aspects), Moscow: Nauka.

Simeoni, Daniel (1993) 'L'institution dans la langue: lexique et pensée d'État', *TTR* 1(1): 171-202.

Slaughter, Frank G. (1960) *Puritans in Paradise*, London: Hutchinson; translated by F. de Bardy as *Amour aux Bahamas: Les pèlerins du paradis*, Paris: Presses de la cité, 1962.

Snell-Hornby, Mary (1988) *Translation Studies. An Integrated Approach*, Amsterdam & Philadelphia: John Benjamins.

Stackelberg, Jürgen von (1971) 'Das Ende der 'belles infidèles' – Ein Beitrag zur französischen Übersetzungsgeschichte', in Karl-Richard Bausch and Hans Martin Geiger (eds) *Interlinguistica. Sprachvergleich und Übersetzung. Festschrift zum 60. Geburtstag von Mario Wandruszka*, Tübingen: Max Niemeyer, 585-96.

Stein, Dieter (1980) *Theoretische Grundlagen der Übersetzungswissenschaft*, Tübingen: Gunter Narr.

Steiner, George (1975) *After Babel: Aspects of language and translation*, Oxford & New York: Oxford Univeristy Press; 2nd edition 1992.

Tirkkonen-Condit, Sonja (1992) 'A Theoretical Account of Translation – Without Translation Theory?', *Target* 4(2): 237-45.

Toury, Gideon (1995) *Descriptive Translation Studies and Beyond*, Amsterdam & Philadelphia: John Benjamins.

Vázquez-Ayora, Gerardo (1977) *Introducción a la traductología*, Washington, D.C.: Georgetown University.

Venuti, Lawrence (1995) *The Translator's Invisibility: A History of Translation*, London & New York: Routledge.

Vinay, Jean-Paul and Jean Darbelnet (1958) *Stylistique comparée du français et de l'anglais. Méthode de traduction*, Paris: Didier.

Vinay, Jean-Paul and Jean Darbelnet (1996) *Comparative Stylistics of French and English. A Methodology for Translation,* translated and edited by Juan C. Sager and M.-J. Hamel, Amsterdam & Philadelphia: John Benjamins.

Wienold, Götz (1990) 'Typological Aspects of Translating Literary Japanese into German, II: Syntax and Narrative Technique', *Target* 2(2): 183-97.

Wilss, Wolfram (1977) *Übersetzungswissenschaft: Probleme und Methoden*, Stuttgart: Klett.

Wilss, Wolfram (1994) 'A Framework for Decision-Making in Translation', *Target* 6(2): 131-50.

Wyle, Niclas von (1478) Reproduced in Adelbert von Keller (ed) (1861) *Translationen von Niclas von Wyle*, Stuttgart: Stuttgart Verein No. 57; reprinted 1967, Hildesheim: G. Olms.

Zimmer, Rudolf (1981) *Probleme der Übersetzung formbetonter Sprache: ein Beitrag zur Übersetzungskritik,* Tübingen: Max Niemeyer.

Zaitun, Nik (1994) 'The Translation of Shakespeare in Malaysia', *Warwick Working Papers in Translation. Cross Cultural Transfers*, Graduate Studies Series I: 93-97.

Zukofsky, Celia and Louis Zukofsky (1969) *Catullus*, London: Cape Goliard Press.

TRANSLATION THEORIES EXPLAINED
Series Editor: Anthony Pym, Spain
ISSN 1365-0513

Other Titles in the Series

Translating as a Purposeful Activity, Christiane Nord
Translation and Gender, Luise von Flotow
Translation and Language, Peter Fawcett
Translation and Empire, Douglas Robinson
Conference Interpreting, Roderick Jones
Translation and Literary Criticism, Marilyn Gaddis Rose

Forthcoming in 1998

Contemporary Approaches to Translation Teaching, Donald Kiraly
Translation in Systems, Theo Hermans

Also Available from St. Jerome

Dictionary of Translation Studies, Mark Shuttleworth & Moira Cowie
Western Translation Theory from Herodotus to Nietzsche, Douglas Robinson
Wordplay and Translation, edited by Dirk Delabastita
Traductio. Essays on Punning and Translation, edited by Dirk Delabastita
Method in Translation History, Anthony Pym

Plus

The Translator. Studies in Intercultural Communication, a refereed international journal edited by Mona Baker